MEAT & MILK

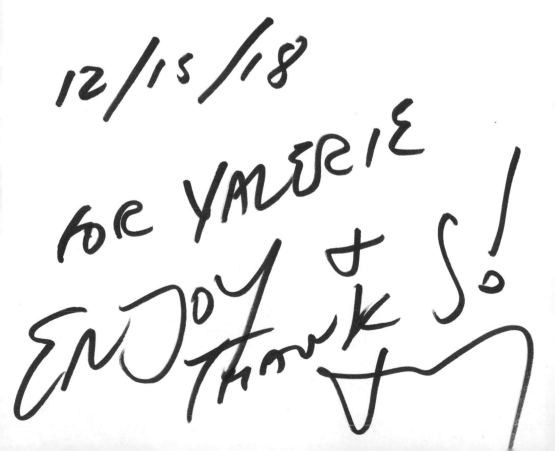

12/15/18

FOR VALERIE

ENJOY Thank So!

PROPS FOR *MEAT & MILK*

"Poets don't usually write poetry. They become poetry. They inhale and exhale metaphors and alliterations like trees give us air. Fury Young is such a poet. His poems are the blueprint of his mind and his soul. His heart provides the passion. For poetry lovers especially this collection of work is an exciting odyssey through this time and space."

Abiodun Oyewole of The Last Poets, author of
Branches of the Tree of Life:
The Collected Poems of Abiodun Oyewole 1969-2013

"Fury Young is a bardic L.E.S. rubble-rouser with a cause, letting his truth flow out with grit and humor and a downtown devotion to seeing and seeking. I remember when I was just a kid with no rhythm Fury put his big old headphones on my head and said now go walk around -- this city feels so good with a soundtrack! His poems are city soundtracks. Mood pieces, dumpster portraits, milky outpourings of fine and furry feeling. Hungry poems clawing towards soul sustenance. Fury is the funky flâneur we didn't know we needed. Impassioned impulsive street wanderer telling it like it is and like it wants to be. These are hopeful and honest songs for our strange sad century: 'And do the heart's fire / And the brain's hard work / And sometimes be a jerk.' Indeed!"

Alexandra Tatarsky, mime/poet

"The Talmud tells us to keep meat and milk separate but Fury Young's poems refuse separation. He says he was an angry young man and gives us the evidence. Still, though there's plenty in the world and in these poems to strike righteous anger, Fury's open eyes and open heart allow all that he sees — streets, subway seats, sad faces, singers and songs — to simmer and shape into life-filled lines of image and sound. *Meat & Milk* gives — not only pages of neatly typed poems — but, also, the source of these poems: the scratches in notebooks, the quotes that spark, drawings and poem's lines. This wonderful book shows 'Misanthrope become poet,' as Fury says."

Judith Tannenbaum, author of
Disguised as a Poem: My Years Teaching Poetry at San Quentin

"Fury Young embodies the righteous anger and energy of the Lower East Side, Bushwick, and other artist's enclaves. He plunges directly into the pain and grittiness of life, like a brutal Chinatown massage. In a time of fake digital worlds, Fury is a scream for the Real, a ghetto visionary; an authentic downtown voice which channels the rage of the incarcerated, survival on the streets, and raw dog sexuality. *Meat & Milk* accomplishes the task of occupying your mind, heart and balls!"

Master Lee, legendary NYC street performer, author of
How To Be An Artist and Not Lose Your Mind

"*Meat & Milk*, the debut poetry collection of Fury Young, is an inspiring chronicle that requires readers to wear the skin of the poet and experience the world the way he sees it. Young is a scribe recording and remixing a full spectrum of experiences of what it means to be alive in this moment, using language both as a weapon and as a shield. With dazzling candor, Young digs into the marrow of his inner being that ultimately instigates a call to action through music and the arts. *Meat & Milk* is full of the stuff of the everyday that is woven into a bigger, more ambitious picture. The result is a brew that is gripping, moving, sarcastic, innovative, sometimes hilarious, and often uncomfortable, that will resonate within you as it did in me."

Gabrielle David, publisher of 2Leaf Press

MEAT & MILK

FURY YOUNG

LIT RIOT PRESS
BROOKLYN, NEW YORK

Published by Lit Riot Press, LLC
Brooklyn, NY
www.litriotpress.com

Book and cover design by Fury Young

Names: Young, Fury, 1949-
Title: Meat & Milk / Fury Young.
Description: Lit Riot Press, 2016. | Summary: Meat and Milk is the debut poetry collection of Fury Young, a born and bred Lower East Side NYC poet. | ISBN 978-0-9976943-3-8 (pbk.)
Subjects: BISAC: POETRY / General. | POETRY / American / General. | POETRY / Subjects & Themes / General.

CONTENTS

For Alexander Pridgen, the monolith in the wheelchair

INTRODUCTION
by spoon Jackson, knight of Realness

I met this cat, this poet Fury Young, through my poetry mentor Judith Tannenbaum. I'd met Judith decades ago in a basement classroom at San Quentin State Prison. Judith taught poetry and inspired a whole new world and dimension to my doing time. Until then I was a prisoner who was beginning my journey as a student in life. I read, pondered, and studied books on almost every subject. I had come from the heart of the high desert and had only known small town desert life. I could leave the confines of incarceration for hours, even days, exploring the worlds that books had opened up to me.

I could have continued my journey in silence, with the love of knowledge and growth. I thought poetry was beyond me. The philosophies I read of Emerson, Spinoza, Plato, and Aristotle would quote and refer to poets, but I had never really read or studied poetry until I found my niche in Judith's class as a bard. I thought poems must come from some hidden, magical place, a place heavy with knowledge and wisdom.

Some spirit, muse, or magic moved me to create my first poem one Christmas Eve. Somehow I let go of my pre-conceived notions of what should and should not be. Some force, some sweet realness, engulfed me. The next Monday, I caught Judith in the hallway of the education building and handed her my poem. I had been in Judith's class, shades on day and night, in silence, for over a year. When she read the poem, all she could say – with tear-filled eyes – was "outrageous."

After I began to write, I gradually realized that all my letters back home had been poetry too, that all along I had been writing poems. My life was the melody that flowed like free verse.

14

I eventually discovered myself to be an actor, writer, teaching artist, native flute player, and human rights activist. Over the many years I've spent in prison, I've won four PEN awards for my poetry and writing, and published two collections of poetry and a dual-memoir with Judith Tannenbaum; *By Heart: Prison, Poetry, and Two Lives.*

When Fury first wrote me, he told me he'd read *By Heart* and loved my writing, and that he wanted my participation in a project he was producing called *Die Jim Crow*. Of course the title interested me. I had known of the old Jim Crow laws and how it had affected my people. I had read Michelle Alexander's book, *The New Jim Crow*. As a prisoner in the mass incarceration system of California, I knew and lived first hand how old and new Jim Crow laws are quilted together, and are still in play. As a prisoner who has only been to Barstow and prison, the injustice of the entrenched old and new Jim Crow stands out like a high desert sun in July.

Over the many years I've spent incarcerated, Judith has referred several people to me: activists, artists, professors, teachers, and young folk who were looking to do projects on the justice system, arts in prison, or just to gain some enlightenment from someone incarcerated. My relationship with Fury has stood out. I would eventually come to know him as a fellow poet, but my earliest recollection of our creative collaboration is with *Die Jim Crow*.

Fury wanted to use some of my poems, prose, and flute playing in his project. This was fine with me. But he wanted me to sing over the phone and have that recorded as well. I have been told more than once I have a bluesy voice that could curl toes. Yet, I have never sang in public or to anyone before. Nor did I think I would ever be recorded singing.

I had no problem reading my poems and prose and playing my native flute over the wall phone in the dayroom at Lancaster State Prison. Fury recorded across the line in New York. He also kept heat on me to sing. I had learned in prison years and years ago, that to grow and avoid monotony and staleness, I must keep my mind, heart, and spirit open to new ideas and ways of doing things.

I started to sing in the dayroom over the landline phone, often with other prisoners on the wall phone next to me. Some prisoners passed by as I sung. I sung for countless hours over many weekends. The main poem I sang was "No Beauty in Cell Bars." I never felt totally comfortable or confident singing, but I did it.

I told Judith about my singing and she laughed and wondered why I never sang for her. Fury, finally, figured out that I am not a singer, and that he could secure better prospects from prisoners gifted in that art form. Perhaps, if I had started as a kid, I could have been a blues cat. I thought the idea of me singing was absurd and yet cool. I learned quickly that Fury had a lot of nerves.

We need folks out there in the world with nerves. Especially artists, activists, and teachers, to stand up and speak out like a bullhorn about the injustices; the Jim Crow of old and new, the sexism, racism, abuse, hate, and mass incarceration. We all must find or create a human way to be human.

This past July, Fury came to visit me at Lancaster. I destroyed him in a couple of chess games. Fury won – almost won – at Scrabble, but time ran out on the visit.

We discussed how focused he was on his project *Die Jim Crow*. I appreciate steadfastness, people who stay focused and put in the hard work to accomplish a goal. People who keep their word. People who dare to fail. When you dare or take a chance, you always learn something.

The same dedication, passion, and empathy Fury unleashed into his *Die Jim Crow* journey, you will find in his collection of poetry, *Meat & Milk*. Realness eats raw meat, and has the staying power of the sun. I feel the realness in his collection.

Fury was denied by security to bring in copies of his poems, so he shared with me a few he had memorized. As he recited "By The Dumpster," the opening piece in this book, I felt his feeling of home there – the smells, the silence, the abandonment.

"Hateful Right Now" depicts how hate, like life, is in the moment. His tortured soul says,

> "All I want to be
> Is hateful
> Right now."

Which leaves hope for love to blossom in the future. Even though he writes,

> "I've spent three years
> Being
> Trying
> To Love"

the one key ingredient is just letting go and being love. Love in the moment, no pondering or trying, just letting go and being; as the voice in "Roxie" tries to do.

> "Kissing you is a conversation
> At the end of the world"

But they have only seen each other in darkness. The deep longing to know love appears in each stanza in this poem, and in stark contrast what follows is "Love Ain't Real." The narrator walks with the rest of us; one foot in darkness, one foot in light.

Poetry is a journey – a complex story, a story that often one must get themselves out of the way to show, so that the poem can forge it's own path, while the narrative unfolds. A full story with a beginning, middle, and end – with a sense of bliss and myth.

You must use the power of the unknown. You must allow the unconscious to rock the conscious. And come up with some horribly deep and fucked up real shit – like being kicked in the gut by a bull – dreams and reality of controlled madness.

Poetry must touch the heart and soul, and later the mind. It takes you to a universal place – a spot inside that is personal and true. It must move the waters of your soul and travel to the mountaintop of your heart. Just like waves in the sea, and clouds in the sky. If poetry does not agitate or make you cry, mad, or warm your insides on a frosty day, then it must go deeper.

Do enjoy the journey of *Meat & Milk* – it takes you deep down into the dumpsters, down staircases, dark alleys, lighted subways, and warm beaches. I close with this poem inspired by Fury's work.

Spoon Jackson
August 2016

CRACK

Back then
You had to have death
in your eyes.
Your voice
must not crack
but sound with fury.
You had to have death
in your walk,
Even if you didn't
mean it.
Swag that showed
you knew
what you were doing,
and death
was like breathing.

@Twitter spoonjackson
realnessnetwork.blogspot-com

WAITING FOR SPOON
is not waiting
for GODOT
CAN'T GODO?
WILL GO ON
MEANS MY GO ON
in my "SAME THING
in my" LANGUAGE

THEY: LET ME in
WITH YOUR SHIRT on
BUT NOT my
POEMS

I thought they
would let
the poems in
because they only

SHARED A FREEDOM
from within
Besides you can
take away the
paper not the POEM
but

YOUNG MAN SHOW 'EM
POETRY IN MOTION
Spoon JACKSON THE actual
FURY A RAVEN
ONE THE SAME
CAN'T TAME CHESS
WISDOM
CHECK

A BACKGROUND

Meat & Milk is my first book of poetry, written over the past five years and parsed out from over three hundred poems and many notebooks. If you had told me five years ago that I'd have a book of poetry out come now, or so many written, it would come as a surprise. I grew up wanting to be a film director. Most of my writing background came from screenplays, and a full length film is what I'd expect to hear as the baby of a half decade's labor.

Take it back ten years to the only formal poetry experience I can remember – a high school English class in which the final assignment was to put together a collection of your poems from the semester. Those pieces are long gone, but on the cover I remember a man running from a crop duster, a la Cary Grant in that old technicolor Hitchcock movie *North by Northwest*. I drew the running man in black and yellow. I wrote every poem in under five minutes and got an A plus from a teacher who I thought hated me. I was a very rude teenager, but I suppose something rang true to her in my words. Though I recall the experience now, at the time it did not stick with me much.

The real birth for me as a poet came at a time when I had no friends, was desperately looking for work, and living in a new place. Sounds typical that the metamorphosis would come from loneliness, and it is, but there were also social events going on around me that I believe propelled my mind into places that only poetry could make some sense of.

As a tribute, *Meat & Milk* is releasing September 17, 2016[1] – the five year anniversary of the social justice movement Occupy Wall Street, which sprang up in New York City, my hometown, a

---

1. The book ended up being released a month later due to further production work, though this was the intended release date!

few weeks after I had moved from the Big Apple to Los Angeles, California.

I was twenty-two and working hard as a film set carpenter and art director in New York. But it was safe, familiar, and I wanted new experiences; to be uncomfortable, to learn, to run away from home. Having gone straight from high school to the workplace, I decided to enroll at the local community college when I got to LA. On a whim, I signed up for a class called "20th Century Genocide."

I would take classes part-time, hoping to be inspired for a script, but I also had to find work. The country was still feeling the reverb of the 2008 market crash, and landing a steady gig proved impossible. I looked everywhere – from Hooters to Chateau Marmont to Pollo Loco – and nowhere was looking for a busboy, a dishwasher, a cashier. My film contacts were all in New York, and the references I'd gotten in LA were unresponsive Hollywood flakes. To make matters worse I had totaled my car in Tucumcari, New Mexico, in a near-death accident on the road trip over from New York. Remember the Little Feat song, "I've been from Tucson to Tucumcari..."?

When Occupy began, I had absolutely no interest in activism. I was a misanthropic and solipsistic teenager who went to a social justice-leaning high school, and I thought the students with their "Impeach Bush" and "End the War" pins were corny. It wasn't that I was a neoconservative rebel, I was just in my own world of Nicolas Roeg, Dario Argento, and Roman Polanski films, with Springsteen, T.Rex, and Marvin Gaye as the soundtrack.

But life was different now. I was out in the world struggling, and my antenna was in a more open zone. Interesting what vulnerability will do to a person.

I stopped by downtown LA's City Hall, where the Occupiers had set up shop. There were hundreds of tents, protest signs, people of many walks, and non-stop interaction around me. I couldn't help being curious and provoked, but that jaded Lower East Side kid who snorted shit coke in dive bars at sixteen wasn't sold. There was still that part of me that lived in a movie. Yet, my receptors were working.

The "20th Century Genocide" class had pulled me in and hit me over the head with an anvil. My teacher was a six foot five army veteran, a black man with long dreads who grew up on a Native American reservation. He'd left the army and become a scholar in history and world religion, while maintaining a staunch atheism. He taught the class like a general with his troops – no bathroom breaks, no latenesses, no bull – but you knew it was because he cared about his students and his subject. He was intimidating, but what we were studying was more so. I was fixed on history, suddenly and without warning. Trips to the Los Angeles Public Library saw me borrowing books by the dozen, and my lonely nights became reading nights, where I pondered deep the tragedies and triumphs of history. I wasn't sure if I wanted to make a movie of all this, and the more I read, the more the idea of turning this history into a film seemed silly. I was reading about the Cambodian genocide, the Holocaust, Rwanda – how could I ever depict that? Why would I? And yet the more I read, the more interested I became in what was going on in the here and now. The more I read, the more I related world history to the present day, and to the country I was raised in.

That's when Occupy became something I wanted to be a part of. I eased my way in with a "General Assembly" meeting, and sat there taking it in, silent, with a Charlie Chaplin-patch jean jacket on my back. On the courthouse steps beside me was a beautiful young woman, but I was too enthralled and shy to say a word to her.

What the occupiers spoke of seemed part-rant, part-truth, part-pain and trauma, but all real. It was a society I had never experienced. Strangers spoke to each other, not with inhibition but with passion and interest. Everything went. People were encouraged to share, which was a stark contrast to the New York City I grew up in, where you wore headphones in public and the typical person did not engage with the interesting stranger on the subway.

Though it took me several more General Assemblies to begin identifying myself as an activist, I slowly started to form these deep questions and opinions about the world around me, as seen through this new lens. Soon I became so obsessed with history and activism that the idea of being behind the camera as a filmmaker didn't feel right any more. A maelstrom of indignant and empathetic feelings hit me, and I dove. I had to live life, to be active in fixing the world's problems: climate change, economic inequality, starving people.

Idealistic? Most definitely, but at least my mind had cracked open. Books I read like Naomi Klein's *The Shock Doctrine* and Loung Ung's *First They Killed My Father* kept me up all night. I'd make collages with Mussolini and the pope and then get frustrated and smash them against the wall of my shabby Westlake apartment. I still didn't have any friends.

Around this time, I started writing poetry. There was no forethought to it. I carried around these heavy questions and thoughts, and when I wrote them down, the poem form came out. One of the first I ever wrote was "By The Dumpster," feeling friendless and in awe of the world. I was sitting next to a dumpster on the Los Angeles City College campus, watching the students and staff pass by. All I had to write with was a thick black marker. I suppose some "sweet realness" came over me, as Spoon might say, and a few minutes later I had a poem. I liked how it felt.

Writing started as a impulse, and it became a means of staying sane; of dealing with depression, dealing with the world's hardest questions, and having some sort of a voice about that world. It's not that studying history and becoming involved in activism made me a poet, but it triggered something that changed the course of my life forever, and in that change a poet was born.

Five years later, here I am surprised that this book is being published. It feels real and it doesn't. I call myself a poet because I am one, not because I've studied poetry or even read too much of it. Sometimes that's the hardest thing – to call yourself something that comes naturally without validation from your peers. In that way this book feels like a gamble, for who knows what the reaction will be? But that's also the fun part. And somewhere there's that fuck-all teenager who says, "Fuck it, these poems are good."

The past five years have seen a lot of change in my life, but one of the constants throughout has been writing. I eventually moved back to New York and my activist pursuits led me to producing the ongoing album project *Die Jim Crow*, a concept album about racism in the U.S. prison system, which several pieces in here are inspired by. There were friends who passed on, lovers met and gone, prisons visited, chances taken, chances not, strangers spoken to, and subways rode.

Meat & Milk is very loosely chronological, and in some ways not at all. Many of the early pieces are just that, and as the book continues, so do certain through-lines. Characters are introduced who you'll meet again, and the journey of life goes on.

Thanks for reading these poems and riding shotgun on this journey. I'll try not to total the car.

Fury Young
July 2016

LUCIFER PRINCIPLE, KILLED MY FATHER, RAPE≠NANKING, VULTURES PICNIC, ECON. CONFESSIONS OF AN HITMAN, SHOCK DOCTRINE, HITLER'S ARMY, PROBLEM FROM HELL (NOT ALL), POL POT BIO[PHILLIP SHORT]("), KING LEOPOLD'S GHOST, LUCKY CHILD, YANOAMA, HOW THE RICH ARE DESTROYING THE EARTH, SOUL ON ICE, IMPERIAL LIFE IN EMERALD CITY, ~~ALL FORCES STATE~~ ALL THE PRESIDENT'S MEN THE RWANDA CRISIS, OCCUPY PAMPHLET, LULU IN THE SKY, PEOPLE'S HISTORY OF THE UNITED STATES, PANTHER BABY, CONFIDENCE MEN, INVISIBLE MAN, STRENGTH IN WHAT REMAINS, Race for what's left, Debt,

Battling ~~nihilistic~~
notlingness ~~less~~ feelings...
feelings of impotence?
Wllat is this all
for, any of it? Sure
I'd rather be doing Oc-
cupy than anything else
here, but why? I mean
what's it gonna do?
~~Does anyone~~ care anymore?

ANSWER: Forge ahead
for now w/ whatever
vague inkling you have.
You know in your heart
what you stand for.

I aint no cool dude
but there's somethin in me
sacred

Why the

chicken

cross the

road?

to hit up the

fried chicken

spot

TELL GANGS and THE SEVENS PLEASE PROMISE ME NO NO

THE THE
EYES EYES
NEVER NEVER
CHANGE CHANGE

By the dumpster
feel alright
there's sawdust in it, an pizza box
cut off pieces of wood
nothing in it is saying anything
by the dumpster
I feel balanced
it's ~~█████~~ rusted and beat up
it will always work
if I could come back as an object
or pick a burial ground
the dumpster wouldn't mind
as long as it had room

I'm just sittin on   some palette
by the dumpster
You could never feel too bad around
and the trash   the
it's pretty accepting   dumpster
like an old mama
         minus the beauty of a woman

BY THE DUMPSTER

By the dumpster
Feel alright
There's sawdust and a pizza box
Cut off pieces of wood
Nothing in it is saying anything

By the dumpster
I feel balance
It's rusted and beat up
It will always work

If I could come back as an object
Or pick a burial ground
The dumpster wouldn't mind
As long as it had room

I'm just sitting on some palettes
By the dumpster yeah
You could never feel too bad
Around the dumpster and the trash

It's pretty accepting like an old mama
Minus the beauty of
A woman

SQUARE ZERO FREEDOM

When I write a poem
There's a revenge for things undone
All the life that don't come out
In the day to day relay race
That wanna be an endless runaway

You hangover
You life thing
You leave a man undone
You call yourself a masterpiece
But you'll never come out in public

Oh the envy that's tainted
To frustration and lip bitten thought currents
That don't make it lovely
To the beach that wanna run smoothly

To another but can't cuz other
Humans wrestling with a drunken
Headache
Daily
Grind
Mind

Tryin' hard to give you passion
The passion that I feel
Or do you think I'm not genuine?
Do you think I've got a notch to stroke?

Piñero
He was a poet from the Lower East Side

The same side where I arrived in June '89
He was a druggie
I'm a whatever
and comparing one to another is another dumb blunder
Would I be free if I were gay but wouldn't even like it
Would I be free if I performed in the subways and venues

I wish I did but wishes don't
Ever come true for real
They morph into thoughts that wave on to a brand new deal
To to to

Ah but true bravery
Is not a lament floating into self-deprecating ecstasy

But tell me
What road would it take
And what sucker would it have to validate
To make a thing recognized as a thing
To look to for answers for
Wisdom or art or
Back to square zero
Freedom

THE JESTER

The jester
To entertain you
Has his own thoughts too
He can't balance them
There is no balance true

He likes to please people
Make them laugh
His ego walks a thin rope
He can't separate his feelings
from his actions
He can't be serious around others
He lacks traction
He likes action

But when he's alone
He's serious and studious
Last night he got drunk because
He couldn't stand his feeling
Jay-Z said Nas was emotional
and that was his weakness
"I guess he was right,"
thought the jester,
"But without emotions you are teethless."

Peep this
He wants to make the people feel before he croaks
Will his ego repeal
Will he turn it to a joke?

He wants to help the world
You know, the starving people
But his ego says hello and bye
Well let it ride
and do the heart's fire
and the brain's hard work
And sometimes be a jerk.

ODE TO A FAT ASS

That woman
With the booty bounce
When she walks
Got me not knowing how to talk
Look at that big butt walk
Oh my (you're)
God
Two planets in orbit
Sting me a horny hornet
Make the middle of me
The the top of me

because i'm crossing a bridge now
because the plant is fixing to bloom
i sang a song on the subway
and walked the above ground tracks home
as the train boomed past me
I sat down and loved
the moment.

I want you to remember
all wild deeds live on
                    Jackson Browne

WITH
A VIEW

There were many times I wondered
when I'd see you again
                        it was Soul II Soul
a club on the ave
right under the elevated train
the soul train yup
the soul train (yeah)

o "Yet he himself embodied
a profoundly American
worldview: that every problem
has a solution, and that
Americans can find it."
    -Vanessa Gezari 'The Tender Soldier' p2
Is there peace to be had
in a modern city? More
modern more sleek more
buildings more expensive

---

in no order   4.14.13

"I wanted to see an old friend
but didn't have one to see
wanted to see someone who
didn't feel like a politician
I wanted to see someone
who wanted to see me
see someone who was really free
see someone who could make me feel
peace in a city
not lonely or shitty.
I wanted to see someone not too
cool for school
some one who was a kind of wise
not one to disguise, with fire in eyes

IN NO ORDER

I wanted to see an old friend
But didn't have one to see
Wanted to see someone who didn't feel like a politician
I wanted to see someone
Who wanted to see me
Someone who was really free
Someone who could make me feel
Peace in a city
Not lonely or shitty

I wanted to see someone not too cool for school
Someone who was a kind of wise
Not one to disguise
With fire in eyes

And at that moment I knew I was too sensitive
Knew that I had reason to live not competitive

Old friend, where did you go?
And did you know that I never let go.

I wanted to see someone who wasn't on facebook
Someone who lived in the moment
Who wasn't hopeless
or a chauvinist

Someone who didn't talk shit.
Never been locked up but times feel fresh off a bid
Walking down these streets of Manhattan
How outside though not inside
A cage

Many people think they're very cool.
Thank you the Natives who came into cafe today
I'd forgotten people can be soulful spontaneous and alive
Not slaves to the daily grind
or slaves to the daily mind

They say you can't start a fire without a spark

And you were a friend you're lucky to meet once in a lifetime
My heart goes to those out there blocking the pipeline
I'm picking my nail skin cuz I like how the pain feels
I am a farmer your crop is my main yield
Is my feelin' for you like pickin' this skin?
An unnecessary habit too hard to kick
A girl like you how could you not find love again?
You're the most lovable woman who I ever met
A voice like a mediation bell or am I being idealistic
And this be a boy who's mostly pessimistic
I was by your school today I felt your vibe
If you're taking in the words please know you're alive
Say to yourself "I'VE FOUND MYSELF LIVE
AND BECAUSE I'M HERE I WILL GROW LIKE IVY."
And I want the world to know in case I might go
That treading forward is how I did row
And for all of the questions I answered a handful
That people ain't honest enough
That one's for damn sure
Biological diversity
is essential to life.

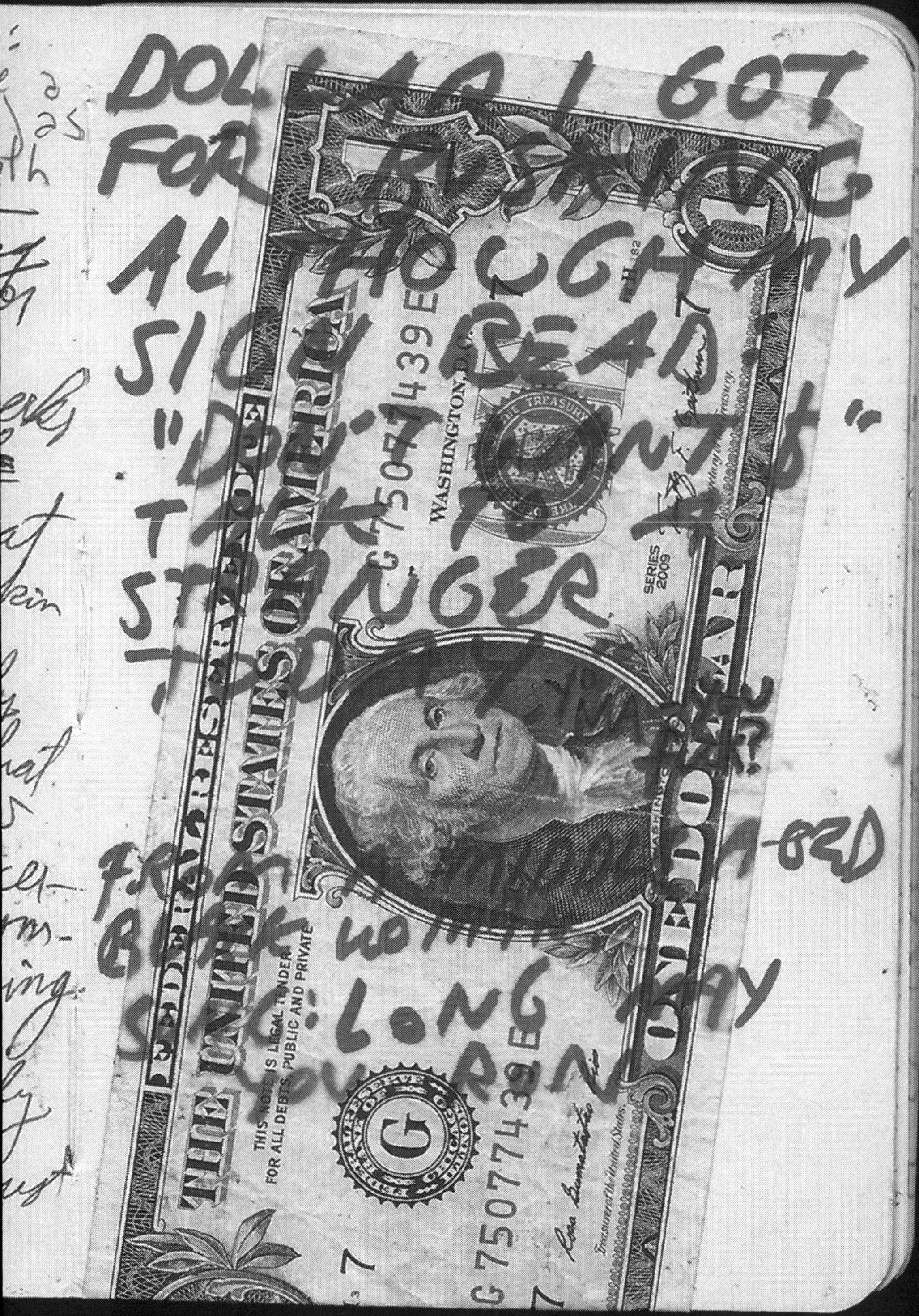
DOLLAR I GOT
FOR BUSKING
ALTHOUGH MY
SIGN READ
STRANGER
BLACK WOMAN
LONG MAY
YOU RUN
THE UNITED STATES OF AMERICA
WASHINGTON, D.C.
SERIES 2009
THIS NOTE IS LEGAL TENDER FOR ALL DEBTS, PUBLIC AND PRIVATE
G 75077439 E

ZAFRA, a pretty name, means har- vest. Zafra Zafra Zafra Zafra

- LONG MAY
- WON'T BACK
- WALK LINE
- TWIST/SHOUT
- FISH WHISTLE
- HELLO IN THERE

"ONE must always do what Satan forbids. What other cause do you think that I have for drinking so much strong drink, talking so freely, and making merry so often, except that I wish to mock and harass the devil who is so wont to mock and harass me."
- Martin Luther 1530

che in four minutes; timed.

FLIPSIDE

Wanting to be a guerrilla fighter
Wanting to be a revolutionary
Writing poems in my sleep
Petrified by the light of day
Guess I like being in control
Fuck it, who's got soul?
I'm really the shyest person in the world
That's why I loved Amanda
But I'm a Gemini so if you believe in that shit

I am the flipside
Dick ride
Don't fuck with my wavelength or do because that's what life is
Too many people sometimes to feel peaceful
Big fish small pond — but we're all equal?

YOUR LOVE IS THE
BERMUDA TRIANGLE
YOUR HANDS LOOK LIKE
A COOLIE'S
YOUR LOVE IS A GYROSCOPE
I DREAMT WE HAD A
HAPPY REUNION AND ENDING

YOU HAVE FUN TITS
THEY CAPTURED ME
BLINDFOLDED I
PUT ME 10 FIRING SQUAD
AND PARADED ME WITH
BLANKS.

THEN I THOUGHT ABOUT
YOUR NEW LOVER
AND DREAD FLED MY HEAD
HIS CUM ON YOUR CHEST

il may have to portray
myself in Film, in order
for it to be clear and
sensically cerebral - in
other words the feelings

THE BERMUDA TRIANGLE

Your love is the Bermuda Triangle
Your hands look like a coolie's
Your love is a gyroscope
I dreamt we had a happy reunion and ending

You have fun tits
They captured me
Blindfolded I
Put me to firing squad
and paraded me with blanks.

Then I thought about your new lover
And dread fled to my head
His cum on your chest

SENTIMENTO

After walking a hundred miles
She still wanted to drift
She carried a flag
The pole was bamboo
She was too strong for

He was stupid
Listening to The Cure
"Pictures of You"
Like when he was in ninth grade
Making up a love to miss
Now he had one to dismiss
Because their

She watched a carousel
He walked the bridge
All graffitied up
And wondered if the city's budget was tight
She was having a new boy

He was senti
ment
No – or so
He tried to tell himself

They were both raised by parents who were still together
Probably his were happier
Yeah

In grade school she pulled a kid by the hair
Knocked him off his chair
When he bullied her for being Chinese

She told him in bed
Both naked and early in their twenties

In Cambodia there are no exact birthdays

She laughed when she told him
For she was rarely mean
To pull down the bully
He smashed his head
And bled
She

He watched a video
She was on a flat escalator
The lights behind her changed color
"Don't move your face,"
He directed
It was his personality

She broke her bamboo flag
She knew more how to
Swallow pain
or
to not communicate it
She had a twin sister
She had a sweet profile
She was bowlegged
Her hair looked like wind
She moved like an undiscovered species
She reminded him of a little girl sometimes
She was never going to see him the way he wanted her to again
She loved making art
He knew that was the most important thing to her

And he was just a malleable piece of dust
And he wanted to be a hard man
Because he was a hard man
And he needed her softness

He had had a good life
He cried today for eighty seconds
Reading about the Vietnam war
In a People's History of the United Rape

Wondered,
"I guess I'll just hold on
and be happy with the friendship we did have
and not think about it
too much."

But like this
There was no ending
So shoot it in the head
And call it a dog dead.

after walking 100 miles
she still wanted to drift
she carried a flag
the pole was bamboo
she was too strong for

He was stupid
listening to the Cure
pictures of You
like when he was in
ninth grade
and making up a loser
to miss
now he had one
to dismiss.
Because their

She watched the carousel
he walked the bridge
all graffitied up
and wondered if the city's
budget was tight
she was having a new
boy

And an accordion chided the lake
A friendly funny complaint
of life

And I swear a woman passed and said,
"What a cute dog!"
Lookin' right at me
And a branch lying on the cocaine said nothing
But felt a lot

And a smooth booty passed
And a few Cambodians
And we remembered the days
When life was old fashioned

A passin' baby screamed cuz he wanted more rations
and had to pee
His having to pee rubbed off onto me
Me n' the dead dog in unison let a yellow river roam

AIN'T SEEN A MOVIE

A wise one once told me
The closer you get to truth
The more unhappy you become
But that wasn't a wise one at all
That was me

Ain't seen a movie in months
Used to want to make them
Something changed in me
I realized I had to live life

I write poems so they'll know
My heart was true
But poems don't speak loud enough

GORGE OF AN OPEN SKY

One day I'll write a poem
About bristling satisfaction
I might be somewhere with a gorge
Of an open sky

Cotton candy and orange
And at that moment I connect with anyone
As comfortable and easy
as warm water

I might be in a subway
Dirty with a fat rat hide and seeking
As long as I can share that affinity
With life I'll be happy

And no one'll know I hit it
But they'll be okay with my presence
That stranger yeah a stranger
and perhaps even welcome my presence

I won't fear my fellow man
My fellow woman, I won't fear them
Dare I say these strangers are sacred
But make me feel naked

And he realized he was calm
He was an ocean in his heart
We're all nature but it's hard
To feel it surrounded by artifice

N' I remember that night in prison
when Marcus told me where he was from
And at that moment if love never met me again
Which was fate
Life would be alright

regret what and live what
love many or few
or all
have a ball or be a ^mounted stuck loser
ask who on a date
to ^and who to ~~on a duel~~ be in love or in hate
or nowhere in between!
how nice how mean
dirty clean ~~fit~~ ~~team~~
on what dream team all up
with a scheme

I saw you chillin on the moon
you were eating unicorn meat
sitting on the lip of a crater
dipping the head in cheese
sucking love gravy out of the horn
licking your fingers with the succulence
of a peasant's banquet
there was food all over your mouth
you wiped it off and ate it
and the beat kept going
now we were ~~swing~~ horns started blowing→

UNICORN MEAT

I saw you chillin' on the moon
You were eating unicorn meat
Sitting on the lip of a crater
Dipping the head in cheese
Sucking lava gravy out of the horn
Licking your lips with
The succulence of a peasant's banquet

There was food all over your mouth
You wiped it off and ate it
And the beat kept going now we were rowing
Horns started blowing
I forgot ey'thing I was knowing
I bowed down to your ocean
Awoke from dream

"GIRLS WEAR SKIRTS"

I'm regenerating
and I got no thoughts at all now
None that'll get a blind man out a cave

Someone, take my arm
Just grab it
Don't ask why
And direct me
Massage the levers of my inconsistent courage
With the knowledge of a herder
Sage, cream, a chicken, and mushrooms
You could be a man, I don't care
The love of a brother could foster a father

Today was the first warm day in awhile
Skirts that preempted summer
Lovers who'd met in winter
Basked in sun removing each other's splinters
And looked at the beautiful passerby

Thinking should I stick with the one on my arm
But as the sun lied to the earth
Most went home together.

There goes the brother I've seen for years in the hood
Young dude, pushing 'cross the street fast in that wheelchair
Angry
Looking on headphones

And there goes a sister
Most stackingest ass I've seen today
Hey
She's walking like a monolith.

Yeah most of the lovers went home asunder
But not many broke through thunder

Once I loved a woman who told me
"Girls wear skirts when they wanna look sexy."

THIS CITY'S INVITE ONLY

This city's invite only
and the politics are on a charm offensive
Who's that bad ass chick with the bad ass tattoos?
Did she earn them?
What do they stand for?

MIGUEL PIÑERO'S
LOWER EAST SIDE

Miguel Piñero's L.E.S.
is long gone.
Damn Mikey.
It is what it is right?

The rawness of your days
are just paid homage to now
in photographs in hotel lobbies
and boutiques that took over venues

"DIE. YUPPIE. SCUM!"

It's like money is a tidal wave, Mikey
And if they scattered your ashes on the Lower East Side
no one would really care
Don't scatter mine there

There's still bodegas on B C D
Projects by the river
Just surrounded by condos now
Ain't the faggots and freaks really no more
Pimps' bars n' juke saloons

I don't know man was born
the year after you died
on Eldridge, Delancey and Rivington
Lee Q. sprayed and Wong painted you
A gun shooting
Full heart moon ricochet!

Where Pridgen sat and fed the pigeons
outside AIDS patient nursing home
Now that's goin' down
condo goin' up

You know baby I want
To keep the flame alive
Represent you
Represent those ashes

Scattered on Ridge
Eldridge A to D
1st 2nd 3rd
St. Mark's Rivington
Norfolk and Clinton

Where my great grandpa's poultry shop was
Tante Rosie's One Day Old Bread
Where Babbi and Zayde got married
Yeah them Jews and Puerto Ricans
Them Blacks Chinese Dominicans

Yeah I wanna represent something
But it's gonna be broader Mikey
Because shit evolves n' devolves
Because shit changes

Will be what L.E.S gave me
What you gave it.
So come down Piñero
Havin' a party like Sam Cooke
Got the black woman with the blonde wig on
Yeah she's havin' fun man

Miguel Piñero,
Let's go.

ODE TO A PIGEON

The pigeon did not have a terrible life
Though it walked in a limp
It's toe was cut by some human-placed spikes
On a sill, it's former perch

It's orange eyes
It's tidal coo
These were things that comfort it's lover
It's teal purple neck
And pink little talons
Were always movin'
Like the folk around it

In a city somewhere
it surveyed the grounds
Felt a shit, let it out
Vacuumed a scrap, conquered a bath
And when no one was looking, took a nap.

TRAP

I don't know if it was the city streets that got me
Or my past life avoiding the wrath of toddler nazis
But something caught me
Made me feel locked in

Locked in like the trap of a mouse cuz a' swiss cheese
Locked in like a nun on his knees giving head
Locked in like Elvis ain't dead he's alive and still manic like a
    motherfucker
Your brains is a manic lover
That's the shit that I be on
I took myself to senior prom.

RUBBER DUCKS

Waiting for a talk about a safe house in Nepal for child prostitutes
Had sex last night
First time in months
To ejaculate is fantastic but with love is more drastic
The ejaculation is like getting shot in the head dead

Prior to that you're in a maze
A maze of love or maze of lust?
With a stranger,
A maze with feigned trust

I am an intimate mother of fuck
And do people just
Fuck for the feel?
Or do they fuck because they want to feel real?
Real is a pussy and real is a cock
Real is an asshole and real is a flock

Of pigeons flying high in the clouds
Circling together and lookin' real proud
You were caught in a genocide and looked at the birds
They told you where the dead bodies were and that's where you
    veered
You hid under a bed in slaughtered hospital
Militia man walked in
Peered around didn't find you
That was it

Your heart was in your neck
Further –

In your head
Your heart was a racing mouse
I DON'T WANT TO BE DEAD

Something lighter

My dad likes rubber ducks
They're all over his bathroom
They're on the shower curtains
Ducks on the bath floor

Ducks holding soap
Ducks sniffing dope
Ducks choking rope
A rubber duck, Tweety Bird too
My dad is gay
And so are you

As a kid
"Gay" was like nigger
Do people need that word,
That makes another shiver?
Eh

To write out of nerve is to ball someone you don't love
It feels good but you don't feel the passion Sisyphus felt with that
    boulder
You son of a bitch, stop being shouldered.
You silly little rabbit, get up and GO FORWARD.

But I'mma contradict myself and say something backward
That something out of nerve has an urge that is awesome
And you are a blackbird whose good luck has blossomed

your heart was in your
further — in your head
your heart was a scin—
I DON'T WANT TO —

something lighter

my dad likes rubber ducks
they're all over his bathroom
they're on the shower —
ducks on the bath floor

ducks holding soap
ducks shitting dope
ducks choking rope
rubber ducks tweety
my dad is gay, and
as a kid
"gay" was like nigger

do people need that wo—
that makes another sa—
Eh
to write out of nerv—
is to ball someone you
it feels good but you don't
felt carrying back up

neeke

mouse
RE DEAD

sing

his too
are you

er?

don't love
feel the passion sisyphus
the boulder

HONKIN' BITS

"Dey call me Honkin' Bits
Dey sayed I was derelict
But boy dem boys is licked.

I be pickin up pick up sticks
Hey now I be ain't rich
Hey boy I be real slick
I ain't poor either
Even though me bank stay zilch

Oh for sure I'm da biggest mensch
Even got me a powerful wrench
I'll rub a boy out in a minute
"Smack 'I'm" over de head
With this wrench yeah I did it.

I did this I do this with me eyes closed
N' you call yo'self truth in a blindfold?
Ye I'm talkin' to you justice!
I don't
Want repairin' or a new trials
I want my buddies to come home!
Let me guys n gals out de slammer oh!

Yeah, that's my word
I'm Honkin' Bits."

BOWERY STAIRS

walking up bowery stairs
bullshit man
ha ha ha

BULLSHIT!
homeless wizard
walk down

STOP SELLING ME

Dear world
Stop selling me
I don't wanna compete
The jig is up
I don't want to stare at no screen

Don't want to praise a man named Jesus
Bet he was a good man
Probably a great one
But I'm not gonna hold on to his name

And don't think he'd want me to either

Don't wanna label no person a thug
Until I know what they done
Because if you grew up like them
You'd take the money and run

It's always crucial that one keeps their ear to the streets
That you don't desert your hood
You know what's going down on the ground

That's where the struggle is
That's where the pain is
That's where the beauty is
Nameless or famous

And this isn't just some rhetoric
Nor exactly love thy neighbor
Just a hello to the millions of strangers
Who I've passed and not glanced

ASYMMETIC BOSOM

She had sought the most complicated truths
In the search for something simple
Not simple as dull
But simple as nature
Not the molecules inside it,
But the function of it

She let her thousand human thoughts into one core feeling

That was this
And she is me
She's you when you go home
To a bed or as a mole in the subway.
She sometimes wondered what life'd be without solitude
If constantly constantly you were surrounded
Once she had a lover who lived with her
She couldn't stand it

She had to be alone she needed that abandoned
Feeling on an island

The world was a complicated place and then it was simple
Certain people think of everything politically
Certain people think of everything biblically
Certain peep think ey'thing shits from the
Asymmetric bosom called history
Certain people are in solitary confinement
Others famous others violent
If there were dozens yes-women around you,
Would you become a tyrant?

In following where the line went she walked through misalignment
Saw buildings tall and millions to rent and shanties on the island
Pondered in her big old head is the question of equality timeless?
Am I idealistic but that don't matter
I'll shatter the chatter that batters these answers

That makes me doubt this mental bladder
That sponges that squeezes
That picks up where the grease is
That is fiendish
That holds weight like a demon, a penis

But into the deep end is where you will dive
Into cold water
And you'll adapt in two seconds.

EASTERN STEEL

Today went to the metal warehouse
of so many sheets and tubes
It was dark and huge
In the chambers where it lay
And the workers only spoke as many words as the metal

What needed to be welded
What needed to be cut
What needed to be served
Life so heavy
For some it's light
But cuz it weighs for some
It weighs for all
Like that metal in those chambers
Of darkness and drywall ceilings
Unpainted but patched
Weight all around them

I can't spell it or say it in any other language
Just cuz you're alive life is heavy
Because two million people died
Life is heavy
In two months in Rwanda
A few jungles away
The center of Africa.

Fell on a
The Last
Wrote it on
shocker
hot sauce
on everything electric and
Red   bright
the color of fresh
Please avoid in tro
I'm   tight
I got   a pick

and   a thread
plucked
Please cleavage
cleavage cleavage.
of your soul
like a paper plate
this ain't waste
boots
stomp

FACE ON A PAVEMENT

Face on a pavement
The Last Punk Rocker
Wrote it on a paper plate
Shocker shocka

Hot sauce
on everything electric and
Red bright
The color of fresh
Blood tonight

Please avoid intro
ducing me to this man
I'm tight
I got a pick up on this guitar
And a thread is
Plucked

Cleavage cleavage
of your soul

Like this paper plate
This ain't waste

Boots
Stomp

pavement
Punk Rocker
a paper plate
shocka

blood tonight
ducing me to this math
up on this guitar

is

CUM SHOT N' WONDA TWAT

I was hangin' out with Cum Shot Charlie
n' Wonda' Twat Wanda
Goin' to the freak show
My life is really deep throat
Hallelujah beast mode
North south west east coast
Places I be spannin'

Charlie n' Wanda fit a lot in their cannon
I'm wearin' a thief's clothes
some guy we spent the night with
name I think's Frankie Free Throw

Can you believe this guy gave us free dope?
Spent the night passed out on Wanda's tits
When I woke up so did Charlie's bread
I ain't talkin' bout no yeast though

Oh Cum Shot stop
gettin' it on the fur collar of Frankie's little sister's pink coat
Alright already, said Charlie blinkin', I won't
Twat Wanda laughed
He was just prepping for the freak show
Their act so dynamite made a nun paint her teeth gold
Man I'd tell you more but then I'd violate the street code.

HOW MANY LICKS

Ninety percent of people are all talk
Doppelgängers are all around me
Every day one
Will disappoint.

"...But when you know that you've got a real friend somewhere
Suddenly the others are so much easier to bear..."

I didn't need awful parents
To have a misanthropic bible
But a comrade's heart.

Viscous individuals
With flows like cold molasses
All these interactions 'round me blind dates of a mismatch pair

So many tools
To cater the ego

The porno with Jessie Rogers getting f'ed by a machine
flowing lava
The cell phone social network
Status update and flashy kicks

I'd burn it all,
But how many licks...

END OF SOLACE

Can't stop banging a drum
Cuz that's what humans do
Always between it's gonna be okay
but
And it's not all gonna be okay
You know what I mean?

And all I love is sunlight and music.

So let it shine, sing
but if you sing make it good
and maybe don't at all.
Just let the instrument

Oh and don't make false promises
Tryna' unfuck a fucked up mess
But everyone's fuckin' with me
I see them from the corner of my retina
intrigued

Beware
All eyes on me
It's the end of solace.

UPTOWN TRAIN
RAINY DAY ANGEL

How do you wake a dormant mind?
Pour a bucket a' cold water on 'em
It's got to be fact
That we humans are haaaard to wake

Whether it's four in the morn like now
or 1907 in the south
a white man
Sometimes you've got to pour a bucket
of cold water on 'em
Make us rise

A guy got on the train the other day
Recited a spoken word poem
It was from the heart
'bout trials tribulations
Lots of humility lots of passion
"Donations of just a smile are welcome...."
And in case you're wondering Society
if he was in rags no he wasn't

When he was done reciting
everyone sat there frozen
"Come on guys I don't get any love?
a smile, props, a dollar...?"
So I started clapping
yeah I too had been victim
For that moment there just observing
Then instant. in sync. applause

"Thank you..! See it's not that hard –
What you all are sad cuz it's a rainy day?
You're gonna let the weather dictate your mood?
Shit man, come on people –
We gotta start working together.

You just think 'I'm in my own world
Let me only worry about me.'"

There's a moment of expression
acknowledgement of a hero
doing something to liven
ground zero then back to the grave.

Man how hard is it to get people woke?
Yeah, and myself included!
How hard is it to get people to speak up?
And to acknowledge that –

conversation
RAW
skills
TALENT.
are
LAWS
lacking
CHANGE!

NEW SHIT ON THE BLOCK

You half alive blues wrench
You 9 to 6 chunk a' shit
Mundane casserole
Might as well live in a fuckin' suburb

And the world IS gonna go to shit
Because YOU didn't raise your voice up.

!

NO SUCH THING AS GREATNESS

And I can't write a poem because life is too real right now
And imagine an existence so hostile that a boring but nice person
    was a godsend
Oh god no
No dog don't
There's rats in this garden yeah you better believe they come out
    at night

They play hide and seek and the streetlights just shut off like a dead
    firefly
I wrote the poem and the woman with the beautiful ass walked by
And in my moment of supposed solemn concentration
I felt an impotent wildness to live right now with no abandon

To take a chance at getting a big round ass
Tonight
And fuck all my exist
Stencil emergencies.

All my attempts at being clever
Went to waste
And I awoke in a pool of semen
From the man upstairs' demon

Is poem good without a focus
Is a rhyme cheap hocus-pocus
Am I a giant or minor coward
And there must be NO SUCH THING AS GREATNESS

In
one person.
Yeah all these gods devils revolutionaries
Soldiers rockstars martyrs are just emergencies

That don't mean you can't look to them,
don't mean you can't do something great
But it's why I'm weary of fame
It's why none of this is a game
It's why I'll never be tamed
It's why I'll always be shamed
It's why there is rain
NO
That's cheap that's
just egotistical heresy and steering

But now I am focused again and I'm basically saying
Ahhhh you figure it out
You should be listening.

THE POET IN ME

The poet in me
was the misanthrope in me
the lover in me
the loner in me
the

~~HHT~~ IIII

What do you do
trapped in the literal world
today you hit the bottle
tomorrow you hope it's gone
the null.
The seagull
which just plopped next
to you
is so pompous and plain
only got two legs
didn't need two more
stranger seagull,
I love you
"more" than these stranger
and like humans
these stranger humans
I could never come up

FOR A SEAGULL

What do you do
Trapped in the literal world
Today you hit the bottle
Tomorrow you hope it's gone
the null

The seagull
Which just plopped next to you
So pompous and plain
Only got two legs
Didn't need two more

Stranger seagull I love you
More than these stranger humans
And like these stranger humans
I could never come up and touch you
You'd fly away

I'm sitting on a bench
on the beach
community college campus
This seagull's gettin' rained on
Seagull what do you want?

Food?
Do you know prejudice
Do you know cruelty?
Have you ever had your heart hurt?
Have you committed crime?
Have you written a dissertation on why the sea is sublime?

Have you enjoyed a woman
Have you thrilled a man?
Have you ever studied people and laughed to yourself?
Were you there at my burial
Were you there at my birth?
Do you get depressed like I do?
Do you love the planet Earth?

Do you like the taste of molasses
or prefer a salty meat?
What music perks your wings
Draws milk to your teat?

PEACE

The sunlight, love, colors and food
Nature and animals, conversations which stir
A connection with a stranger
A book that's good, an orgasm
A sacrifice

PRIDGEN

He was born in Harlem
Spent his young years there
eight moved to Melrose Projects
One Fifty Third Street and Cortland Ave
281, 281, 281

His mother had thirteen kids
Daddy Oscar was a killer
With a purple heart from the second world war
Left the family some point or another

His mother went down Orchard Street
the Lower East Side
Knew Yiddish and for that
the Jews loved her

He went to Clinton High
Most dangerous in the city they said
Put his glasses in the back pocket
Look cool for his school crush
and there his glasses got crushed.

"Alex — you're not stupid — you just can't see!"

He didn't go to college
Married soon after high school
had a kid with her
selling life insurance
The parties got into using

And many women and eight kids later
He was a dealer and an addict
Always walking a tightrope
But people just trusted him with the money.

'Round then mom got killed in Jersey
She was driving, hit a T-bone
He made a speech at her funeral
That just came to him then and there

It made the house cry
They asked if him if it was written
Praised his oratory

Years later he'd recall it in a cafe
With an utmost dignity and pride
And it was one of those moments
You think all these little lives are something beautiful

Week after momma's smash pop was shot in the head dead
Garbage can 'bout to slam on a guy's head before BAM!
Pulls pistol — DEAD.

Alex Pridgen
Splibby Al the Housewife Pal,
or Dr. Death when you brought crack to Melrose Projects

Said he'd done a quarter of a million dollar's worth
of cocaine and it caught up to him
In '86 slam dunkin'
Was on top of her, became a statue
For a moment
Then collapsed.

The stroke left one side frozen stuck forever
And his home became a wheelchair
Nursing homes, bodega corners

A blow job gave him AIDS
Now he's back on the Lower East Side
Rivington House
Two blocks away mom bargained in Yiddish

Being off drugs slowed him down, the wheelchair too
and he spoke slower, thought slower
But boy telling stories he'd speed up

For those who knew him later
it was hard to judge his past
If he was a dead beat father
His attempted murder

His family didn't really keep up
Maybe they were fed up
He made a new family of relics
and strangers on the corner
Some neighborhood kid named Fury
The pigeons he'd feed and named Larry
Mo, Charles, and Carl
Dumpy and Rhonda
"I could get along with a lamppost."

He'd grace every passerby
compliments they didn't deserve
Children to listen to their parents
"She's the boss, huh? Listen to your motha'!"
Grin wide as a great gorge
Leaned in on wheelchair
Head cocked
Like a chicken sensing feed.

He'd flirt with any woman and use the same ones on the men
"Keep doin' what you doin' — it looks good on you."
"You got nice hair my man...."

To a dog "you call that a dog's life?
Walking around with a pretty girl all day?
And I'm supposed to be mad at you being a dog?
I don't think so pal."

He'd tell stories to those who'd listen
and if you did
Tomes.

Bein' bodyguard to the champ,
Muhammad Ali
"Me and Mr. T"
James Brown backstage with hordes of women
Malcolm truthin' on street corners

On summer cookouts at Melrose Projects
his old friends were happy to see him
Splibby Al the Housewife Pal
who didn't quite go off the deep end

All those gangsters he spoke of weren't at that cookout
They were dead, locked up, or out of state.
Pistol Pete, Country Dave, Billy Mapp
Organized Crime "because he was so organized"
Supafly, Queen Bee, Raymond Hamilton

As for him
"I'm Alexander the Greatest
because I outlived Alexander the Great.

….We come into this world
A humble begging pleading creature
Can't control nothin' –
Can't control our muscles
Can't control our hands.
And you're so uncontrol of everything you beat yourself up.
You ever see a baby beat the hell outta theyselves with they own
    hands?"

LEGFUL OF CHICKPEAS

You're only a person
If you take a chance
It feels good to be part of the game
Hit a home run
Run the bases backwards
Do a fox trot (with your eyes closed)
Continue the puzzle (watch your head explode)
Go inside an orifice
Befriend a frog or toad
Eat a legful of chickpeas
With tomatoes and lemon juice, oil
Dig a grave for an elephant
Feed grass to ten horses
Four black, three brown, two green
I guess you ain't seen what I done seen
But you still can be a part of the game
Come on, you're up next!

JIVE

In the city
Plastic bags are tumbleweeds
Life seems complicated
But it ain't really
All that really matters is vigor
I know you're a young woman and you need room to breathe.

Thank you Spoon for reminding me the importance of hard work
Thank you to the coincidences that made this here good
The highs and lows
that made some songs work
and others don't
Too many embellishments

And maybe even
Thank you shyness
And maybe even thank violence
But prob'ly not

Now amongst this bright light
And millions of people
It's gonna be hard to find room to breathe
But cut the sorrow and flash forward to a happy time
I know it sounds like kindergarten but I told you this was
    simple huh
You're on the middle of your seat because you know you got the
    hunger yeah
And you ain't on the edge of your seat cuz you ain't fallin off of
    nothin'

You write on a guitar cuz you're sittin' on music
Your shyness inhibition is a victim of nothing
You're gonna keep on living
Tomorrow half-shot being golden
So beholden yeah beholden and fuck a rhyme when it's a forced one

Whoa that's puberty speak
Hey you have a rudimentary weep
Got an A plus in the tenth grade for a poem I wrote in three minutes
I was a non-confederate rebel and I wasn't no yankee either

A woman is staring across at me
And I know she's reading my mind now
I'm so tense I'm holding two pens
Yeah and writing with the other

Brother mother no man put asunder
Thunder crack hit the road Jack

She's staring and she knows me and she's black about fifty five
she has a real sweet vibe she's portly and secretly majorly alive
hi five
this train is a brightly lit dive – i'm alive
you know how cuz i'm speaking in jive
Alright.

MEANING OF LIFE

Dave asked me the meaning of life
Last night at Lone Wolf
I said to find as much truth as you want

CASTILLO

They say life is what you make it
Man on these streets it feels like a duck could fake it
20 years ago my brother sis had to earn it
And you can bet
Them crackheads were burning it

This ain't no shit
You can take back home to momma
This is some shit
That's like latkes playing the dozens
Dig this – cuz I am the last of some Mohicans

And get your shoes in that boutique but sweetheart this realness
    ain't leaving
Catch me at Castillo del Jagua
Eating a cubano

TITO

Tito was a man from the hood
He'd have your back in a jam
He'd take that bullet you know
Plus he'd stand for the little guy
Tito wore mostly baggy clothes
Learned to read watching Sesame Street as a grown man in prison

Tito was a loner he said, and that's why he was deep
Tito was nice to any new person, someone he'd just meet
And even if you wasn't a team player
He'd think, "Alright go spread love in your own way."

Tito was the man
In the projects, the ave, the bench
He was a thug and he'd say it proudly
That he'd kill you if you mess
And in his eyes he knew word bond

In his past life he was a troubadour who died in a duel

NIGHTMARE ON LAYAWAY

He didn't wanna write a poem
Cuz he was supposed to be living
But he was caught between tumbling drywall
It had been used and reused
The laborers were all drunk
They got it on the cheap
No they found it on the street

Man and his diet was devil's food cake
Just tired and weary
Weary and tired
Ain't it something when your best friend leaves you
And she was your woman too?
But there was a part you never knew and it's crazy how people can
    change

You know it.
You know your brain ain't at peace now
Usually you do this at peace time but you're a constipated flower
A dandelion tryna' bang a war drum
Why don't you go out and forget me not
He loves me she loves me not
He she Z it's all the same

Progressive movement so the lifer said
And this dead author Henry Miller
Laughed and shrugged and loved and fucked
Parisian whore,
Diamonds in bosom

Man it tried so hard to get to truth but it was impotent this stallion
It was a nightmare on layaway
It was devil's food cake with baloney
No ketchup or mustard

The darkest side of the world is in my head right now

A516-198

Man with weird karma on his head
Walks around with it hovering
He's doing 28 to life
For a life he didn't take
Well I do believe that, okay?

And his mother doesn't talk to him
His brother's doing 25 years for drug possession
And his two sisters ain't talking to him either
Hung up receiver

The man with weird karma stays positive
Some kid from New York and ol' girl tryna' help him
Kid from New York says he's doing an album
'Bout racism in the U.S. prison system

EQUAL AND EXACT JUSTICE TO ALL MEN OF WHAT EVER STATE OR PERSUASION

100 CENTRE ST   CRIMINAL COURT BLDG.

UNDERRATED ADAGE

If you got nothin' to say
Say nothin' at all
Simple thoughts are often good thoughts
I'm a nutcracker from planet earth
Rode in on a two-ton pony
That licked the stars for fun bitch

EGO TRIPPIN' FOR NIKKI GIOVANNI PART 2

You saw you conquered
Your flow was bonkers
You came from Yonkers, the hood part
where people
get shot

I'm gay I'm straight I'm crack rock
and everything in between
The lowest piece of shit on the street

I'm the gum stoned in the pavement forever
I'm sayin'
nothin'
No one knows what I'm sayin'
I'm ancient sacred
The drool from a retard
Endorphins at the colosseum
M.I.A.
Lame

You on your birthday
Introvert extrovert
Runnin' outta room on
a small piece
of paper

Chaser the eraser

OKLAHOMA

Met a Native on the train today
dude was from Sugar Hill
Told me hip hop birthed
when some kids from the Ruckers were talkin' over the beats
An agent saw 'em and so
became the Sugar Hill Gang
The Native was named
Oklahoma

Only Native I've ever met from Harlem
got the human freight at Bowery
He didn't look too interesting
a guy from glance

Yankee hat
baggy jeans
asked him, "You listen to Gregory Isaacs?"
"Who's that?"
"Night nurse….
And what about reggae so addictive like candy?"
He said music could be that way for anyone
don't matter the genre
Turned out he loved classical
Beethoven, Rachmaninoff

made the same song century apart
He was a stuck in his opinions guy
But I liked him
Sugar Hill Oklahoma

THE PRECIPICE

He stood on the precipice
in a million interactions
Of the millions of people
Who attracted to whom?
Would peace be found in the month of

The precipice
Wasn't a fine place to be
If you like balance that is
Is that balance like you if

The precipice
Crossed it at that cafe
Where we talked about music from our generation
And you laughed and laughed and we laughed

Crossed it on that subway platform
Where I sang "Sing that song called Soul Train
Sing that song called Duke of Earl
And don't forget get that Soldier Boy."

The precipice
Yes it's fists
in the air
Togetherness
But it's mostly you
working it out
It's not solace
It could be an orifice.

POEM TO BUSK
(TOO SHY TO 'CITE)

To be unparalyzed
That's what I'd like
To yearn more occasionally
Perform on a moving train
Go to a bar just cuz I feel like it
Like having a small
Adventure

Home, home
Are we all going home?
Roam, roam,
Where should we roam?
Lone, lone
Such a lone ranger
How do we connect
Do we wanna
How do you know
And which comes first
Being down with yourself or down with being social?

I'm an incarcerated rabbi with so many questions
Had a far fetched alibi that's how I got in here
Uh.

Follow me, listen me, if only occasion'ly
I'm 'bout to get off this train and I didn't recite this
So that's it – it's also the end of a book
"This is a Queens-bound M train
the next stop is Knickerbocker Avenue"
There's this thick beauty at the end of here
In heels, gaze the window

Night's tripped now, soon these long suns will be over
And some of us may feel more stuck on the daily grind mind
And some of us will try to unleash their oldest freedoms

Some will get pregnant
Between white lines and yellow lines near stop signs on black and
    grey pavement
Some will make rent maybe one O forbid will go homeless
And be begging on this train
Having served in the circus

I have so much love inside me
and I'm yearning sort of slowly
It's not for wanting someone to hold me it's for wanting to know
    peace
So I said farewell to a tragic and a happy end
ing on that bored me
and I'd already done it
I watched a sparrow hop the tracks and thought take a tip from
    them
I watched a master break his back and said might as well go in

Now some have fallen idols and some just have themselves
What's now a broken bottle was once top shelf
We all have struggled with society whether we admit it or not
We all struggle in society
Admit it or don't

I don't have any tattoos
Guy I know has thousands
And yeah life was still hard after all y'all got out prison

"FREE THE PRISONERS!"
Then why do we incarcerate?
"FREE YOUR MIND."
On dead sparrow's dinner plate.

Had a far fetched I watched
how I got in master break
Uh. their back
Follow me, listeand said migh
cr as well go

MASTER LEE'S OPEN MIC

SUNDAYS @ 8pm

LOOKING GLASS (in the old Goodbye Blue Monday)
1087 BROADWAY, BROOKLYN

"Ey man you have a bles
day and put that work
so we can shoot to the
"THANK YOU USING GLOBAL

→ Now some have fallen idols and
some just have themselves
What's now a broken bottle
was once top shelf
We all have struggled with
society whether we admit
it or not
We all struggle in society
admit it or don't
I don't have any tattoos right
now
I guy I know has thousands
And yeah life was still
hard after all y'all
got out prison
"Free the prisoners!"
Then why do we incarcerate?
"Free your mind!"
On a dead sparrow's dinner
plate.

ant

d
rs—
EL LINK—" LOBOT. ■

MY NAME BE FURY YOUNG
I'M A TOMAHAWK TANK ENGINE
I FEEL ANGER AT THE WORLD
JUST FOR BEING IN IT
I'M A MAGAZINE RELOADED

A FAGGOT
A NIGGER JOYCE
A TRIGGER
A MOTHERFATHER FUCKER

HATRED
IS A FUNNY THING TO WASTE
VOICES IN OTHER LANGUAGES
AROUND ME

I'M AFTER WORK ON A SUBWAY
HATING EVERY OTHER POEM EVER
WRITTEN EXCEPT THIS ONE
I'M MOVING
IN ANGUISH

THAT'S LIKE HATING PRETTY GIRLS
JUST FOR BEING PRETTY
N U CAN'T HAVE ONE
HA, YOU SILLY RED HEN

YOU'RE IN YOUR WORK CLOTHES
NOT YOUR PLAY CLOTHES
HOW COME THESE SPILLS
ARE SPEAKING CHINESE?

HOW COME MY HEAD FEELS

...EAK IN THE KNEES
...OULD IT BE THE DENATURED
...ALCOHOL SATURATED IN MY HANDS
...F THERE WASN'T THIS SUBWAY POLE
...HERE WOULD I REST MY WEARY HEAD
I SLEPT 15 HOURS LAST NIGHT
...ABY I'M TIRED AND I AIN'T
GOT A BABY NO MORE, TRULY
A FEW OF THESE THOUGHTS
...RE THEY TRANSPIRE LIKE MAGGOTS
JUST TRYNA FEEL CONTENT
YA KNOW
JUST TRYNA FEEL ONFIYAKNOW?
BUT DOG DAMN DAT'S SO
FUGGIN ONCE IN A WHILE
YAKNOW?
YOU CRIED WHEN WE MADE
LOVE
BUT DAT'S CUZ YOU'RE NOT
GONNA STAY WITH ME
NOW THAT I CAN STANCE
DO YOU LOVE ME

4/1/18

MY NAME BE FURY YOUNG

My name be Fury Young
I'm a tomahawk tank engine
I feel anger at the world
Just for being in it
I'm a magazine reloaded

A faggot
Nigger kyke
A trigger
Motherfatherfucker

Hatred
Is a funny thing to waste
Voices in other languages
Around me

I'm after work on a subway
Hating every other poem ever written except this one
I'm kidding
In anguish

That's like hating pretty girls just for being pretty
N' u can't have one
Ha, you silly red hen

You're in your work clothes
Not your play clothes

How come these spics are speaking Chinese
How come my head feels weak in the knees

Could it be the denatured alcohol saturated in my hands
If there wasn't this subway pole where would I rest my weary head?

I slept 15 hours last night baby
I'm tired and I ain't got a baby no more.

Few of these thoughts
Hope they transpire like maggots
Just tryna feel content ya'know
Just tryna feel on fi'yaknow?
But dog damn dat's so fuggin' once in a while ya'know?

You cried when we made love
But that's cuz you're not gonna stay with me
Now that I can dance
Do you love me

MONOLITH IN THE WHEELCHAIR
by Fury and Alex

The monolith in the wheelchair
Perched on the corner
Foot tappin'
Nursing jelly beans and a joint
"The devil's scared of me
He knows I'm gonna go down there,
Burn up hell and kick his ass
He's tellin' God,
'Please don't let that nigga die!'"

The monolith in the wheelchair
Complimented the passersby
Without judgment or a scent of scorn

"How you doin' dear?
See what happens you listen to your angels?"

On the corner of Eldridge and Rivington
Pigeon food, like prison food
pre-paid phone, dominoes in the bag
pigeons fly, people pass, heels clonk
bodega corner, 92 million is the lotto
But neighborhood changed so
Relics on the the corner
Me, the indigenous
And the monolith in the wheelchair

"I was sittin' here wantin' somethin sweet
And here you come along."

The monolith was a timeless mind
Was open to anyone, could get on with anyone
Barely any of them stopped to talk
It wasn't that neighborhood anymore,
You know what I mean?
You know when you feel that?
But here we are changing that
Me in the wooden chair, the indigenous
And the monolith in the wheelchair

Bikers gone by on the corporation's bikes
they paid off the city
swindled their customers
but it didn't cost taxpayers

One of the pigeons
Dancing in circles
And the sparrows came to say hi on that bed of spilled gyro

"Wow.
Now that's what you call poetry
You better publish that shit
That's some deep shit
Let them figure that shit out
That would immortalize me if nothin' else —
Ey man you walk like you goin' to a fight!"

"Hi dark and lovely."

PINK FLAMINGO

You must
Keep performing
You must
Not be a slave
You must
Nourish those in prison
You must
Take apart the train
You must
Keep it thorough too

You will
Not give in to shyness
You will
Not give in to violence
You will
Not give in to the silence
You will
Try to live in the moment
You will
Crush those upon you
Who do not obey their vestibule

You are
Full of love and freedom
You are
Even a little hopeful
You are
I swear you are on the precipice
You are gonna cross it
You are gonna cross it

You are
A beautiful force in public
You are
Drunk in buplic
You said
Love comes from hatred and starvation
And I thought fuck I really agree with that

You are
A very prolific writer
You aren't great, no one is
But you are a fighter
You are not a biter
I mean you don't steal shit and call it yours

You are
Not just a white man
You are
Not just a black woman
You are
Not just a pink flamingo
Ha
You are just a pink flamingo
And I want to hang on your lawn

I am
Coming to the end of the fuck
I am
Learning how to cock suck
I'm talking about making out with a rooster

I am
Overjoyed and prideful
I am
Formerly suicidal
I am
Grateful for the food on my plate

I am
Excited for our date
I am
Writing with a passion and fury
I am Fury Young and that's why I named myself that

I was
A slumlord to a modern pavement
Myself -
And now I'm an erasure of all human behavior

I am
A slave to the somersault
I am alive in summer and licking it's salt
I am
At this moment
Tying my sneakers
Avoiding interaction
With a very pretty young child

I am
Always about to cry
At precious poetic moments
I am
Thinking about a title
Poetic Champion's Compose
I am
A never ending butterfly
I am
An art art artist of the purest kind
I am
Unafraid of that pretentious line
Cuz it ain't pretentious if you really feel it

I am
Not trying to be anything epic
I am

just disabled
Can't put a pen down.

I am going to
take a deep breath

And just smile at that little delight in pink sneakers.

INSPIRATION
for Spoon

You will never know
Where inspiration comes from
Out of all my weaknesses
Comes something in love
And someday the dust will settle on my yin yang

I'll throw up a gang sign
The gang of a lover
The gang sign of a fighter
The gang sign of a lifer
The gang sign of a golden heart
The gang of someone who lived fully
That's old man me
That's old Fury

3/22/16

You will never know
where inspiration comes from
Out of all my weaknesses
Comes something in love
and someday the dust will
settle ~~just a little~~ on my
ym yang
I'll throw up a gang
sign the gang of a lover
the gang sign of a fighter
the gang sign of a lifer
the gang sign of a golden
heart the gang of someone
who lived fully
that's the old man me
that's old Fury.

Spoon Jonson
Knight of
Reminess
P.O. Box Reminess
The universe

NEW YORK

TO:

CROWN TASTY COMBOS

R.i.P. RKW

Cheese Burger
① Sandwich Only | W/ fries & Soda
3.49 | 5.75

Chicken Burger
②

Fish Burger

Double CheeseBurger
④ Sandwich Only | W/ fries & Soda
.99 | 6.99

Double Bacon CheeseBurger
⑤ Sandwich Only | W/ fries & Soda
5.99 | 7.99

Lamb Gyro

Sandwich Only | W/ fries & Soda
.49 | 6.99

Beef Gyro

⑨ Sandwich Only | W/ fries & Soda
5.49 | 6.99

Philly Cheese Steak
Sandwich Only | W/ fries & Soda
.49 | 6.99

Whiting Fish Sandwich
⑬ Sandwich Only | W/ fries & Soda
4.49 | 6.49

⑭ Sandwich Only | W/ fries & Soda
5.49 | 6.99

⑮ Sandwich Only | W/ fries & Soda
4.49 | 6.49

10 Pcs Chicken Rings

⑯ Sandwich Only | W/ fries & Soda
3.99 | 6.99

Spicy Chicken Sandwich

Popcorn Chicken

15 Pcs. Chicken Strips

Chicken Nuggets

XXI

THE WORLD.

ODE TO FOOD

Food you're the most joyous
Sexually pleasing thing on earth

How I will always appreciate you
How I will never waste you
How I will always know
There have been those who starved without you
And do today

Food
You taste different in different places
You taste best when one eats you at ease
In comfort with a friend
A lover, family
Alone

You unite us all
You are absolutely sacred
In your glucose I worship
A god to living things.

QUIT GIVING A BROTHER

Quit giving a brother
Just teaspoons of your love
I want a buffet
More obtrusive than summertime butterflies

To drool on every pillow

TO HAVE A LOVER

To have a lover
To lie naked on a Tuesday evening wandering
In freedom in the world you create
Where truth lies polished
Like a medieval blade
And sex is a heartbeat
And everything entwines

To have a lover
To lie naked in bed
Just talking
And that truth is on every creation's face
And you feel ancient, and newborn, and every ages
And wild, and innocent, and savagely dark
A killer and a lover and a fighter and a sister
And a brother
To have a lover.

SOPHIA ON THE BEACH

The moment I witnessed
Your most natural magic moment
The ocean and your eyes
Became the same thing
And your expression was as wild
As the parolee waves
And you bounced back to the beach
With the wind as your towel

FOR MY DAUGHTER

I feel the road
Ahead of me
Long and solo one
It's yin yang black and white
Kinda tight extra loose

It's one I'll walk with invisible
Future daughter and these black boots on
Show you how to walk these streets
Hold my hand
Squeeze

clap back 'roove

FOR THE PRISONERS

This is for the prisoners
Who are so much more than that
You should be photographed by the first film camera
In the most ethereal and beautiful black and white

For Obadyah
Who speaks with so much pride
His tattoos show the journey of the Israelites
And his hair is long and braided
He looks like a real cool black radical hippie
And there's something ancient about
His persona

Leon
You told me about Obadyah
You hooked that thing up on your contraband phone
Told me "Sartre, Camus, them my mans…"
And that made me shed one tear of exaltment
"Clap back 'rade"
Was how you ended your letters
And you had more creative thoughts than a leopard on acid

Milishia
You were sweet like the dancing frogs in the card you sent me
But you could smell a bull shit from a bull ring away
And you drew many butterflies
And your soul was really one of lightness
I see you take the bits of sun you've got
And run with and run with it

Tameca
I need you on loud speaka
Your accent is thick
Like honey and molasses
Your handwriting is street
And prison hieroglyphs
Which will one day be on a pyramid
Your vision is myriad

Anthony
Big Ant and the quotables
"Yeah it's me again. You know me always bizzy doing something.
It's either legal work or music.
If it ain't that I don't want shit to do with it."
"I love this shit excuse my french."
"I want this to be historic."
"So I'm ready to rock n roll."
"Because I'm not perfect but I'm as good as it's going to get."

Spoon
Spoon, Spoon
How deep is your deepest poem?
How deep is the blue sea deep?
I think at times you must be depressed
But you're still living in clouds
And when low
Your voice is loud
Not in anger but in two simple things you love
Beauty and, of course,
Realness.

Myron
I heard you were the greatest guitarist ever
I'm not even gonna think about that, man
I'm just gonna meet cha
And I'll be curious like going back to ancient Rome
Am I about to meet a guitar monolith?

Angola penitentiary —
A brick just fell off your wall.

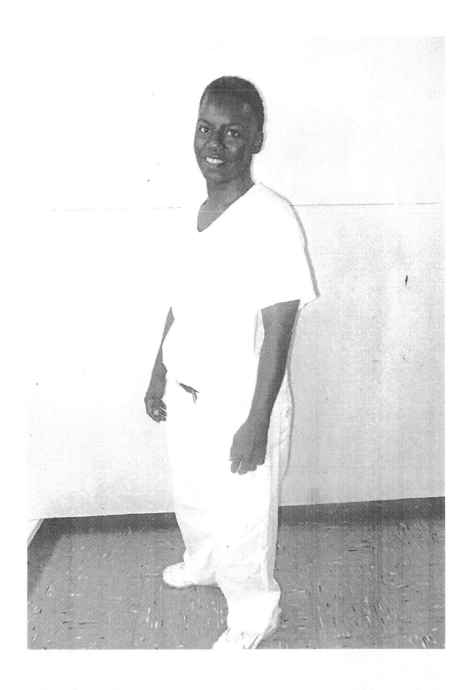

FEW YARDS FROM ANGOLA

The sun is setting
I'm parked a few yards from Angola
I'm just waiting for the visiting hours
To kick in

I'm wondering when
Did time start
I mean when did someone say
"There are hours minutes seconds
and it starts now."

The lifer must be up now

ANGOLA VISIT

I.

Amin Amin
That's his real name
Guy who got LWOP for felony murder
Hung out with him and his mom for hours
after Myron left to go set up the rodeo

Amin kept making jokes
good ones too mostly
was weird he actually seemed happy
Half Italian half "a-rab"
Myron's a restless soul in there
"When I play guitar is the only time I feel alive."

II.

Disconnect from nature.
Disconnect from humanity.
Comfortably numb institutionalized.
Must get far away from here.

I found this land of rusted machine parts
I'm hanging here for awhile
maybe I'll find a motel
to be invisible from these "folk."
Southern hospitality is a lie
Especially amongst the whites

Hell HOT

Kill people
Go ta pen
Life sucks
HUH
Watch tube
Play lotto
Win da jackpot
NOT
Fuck bitches
Beat niggaz
Sling dat mail drop
Catch a body
Life sentence
Oh well
Hell HOT

ASUNDER

Thinkin about my grandmother
After she saw the wolfpack
She was depressed by that
In her happy mind
Made me think that
Everyone got some deep hunger
Something down down there
Something put asunder
Roll of thunder hear my cry

CONTROL MOVEMENT UNIT

i'm carrying a small white rag
this state
sponsored hate crime
life
tryna take mine

supermax
torture chamber
concentration camp

I'm carrying a small white rag
i
Surrender.

Control movement unit
psychological war
low intensity psychological warfare

destroying my senses
destroying my social skills
gulag
gulag
solitary echoes

WHO'S CALLING my name??

Obadyah
obadyah

one day i'll write a poem
about bristling satisfaction
i'll be somewhere with a gorge
of an open sky.

~~inside my 'ed~~

inside my 'ed
you'll see that the joker
is really a loser...
inside my head
the weakest amphibian lies
fetal crevice rock
a cave of inner tormen
carved into some card b
paintings of hell
images of solitary prisoners
kicking in doors
not even human anymore
so far ~~off the deep~~ end
and you couldn't even k
snot hanging like a thread
these are real. tears i've
this is written just for

INSIDE MY 'ED

Inside my 'ed
You'll see the jester is really a loser
Inside my head the weakest amphibian lies

fetal crevice rock
a cave of inner torment
carved into some cardboard
paintings of hell
images of solitary
prisoners kicking in doors
not even human anymore
so far off the deep end

and you couldn't even know it
snot hanging like a thread
these are real tears I've cried
This is written just for me.
to just dynamize an emotion
into the ground
to make it real far away
when I feel okay it creeps up like rat

but it's way more slower than that
it's a snail I want to keep crying
i want to cry away all this
i want to cry like some old love song
i want the snot to be my release date
I want to drive myself into the ground.

DEONTE

I was hospitalized for lead poisoning when I was 2
my sister she died at 3 from the same thing
I grew up in Jersey City, Lafayette Projects
One day my mother and her man got into a fight
she leaned out the window, knocked a flowerpot out
it hit a guy's car, he shot her
She went into my arms, landed dead there, I was 12
My father started taking care of us, an alcoholic
Died of cirrhosis in the liver when I was a couple years older, 15
Lived in foster then my aunt who didn't like me
Stealin' robbin' sniffin' yay
19, armed robbery, put away
Start shootin' up in there
more dope in prison than out
After three was out for a year, went back for two, same charge
Getting more used to the system than society —
I'm out — month later doing ten for attempted murder
Came home '91
OD'ed on junk
I'm back in the hospital where I'm born
Out of the county '99 I'm high
My girl calls my P.O.
said I assaulted her, two more
I'm out in '02
that was it
Never goin' back, never went back.
Now I'm a security guard at City Hall and the precinct
Funny huh
it's a good job though
My daughter 22, she's in college
I'm gonna get married
planning for it to be real good.

MY NAME IS CATAPULT

My name is catapult
All I do is swing
I swing from shadow-filled rooms with empty ash trays & venom
To daffodil forests thick in joy emotion
I got soul

and I'm superbad
But I'm crippled like a seven foot man whose centerpiece is little
Torrid and evangelical that's what Jesus likes to call me
and fuck Jesus
That nigga's played out

Promise that
wasn't for effect
I'm a carpenter too
J sometimes works at the wood shop

Time is tickin'
She's emotion
She's gettin' the best of me
Five minutes pass girl goes from hopeful to hopeless
Tick tock big cock
Cock-a-doodle-doo

O it's a catapult's swan song
It's a lovely little raindance
Now you see how disturbed
I am
A wolf

Wolf, wolf!
That boy cried wolf!

THE CRACKHEAD

The crackhead said to the thief
I can control this.
My 15 beamed up, man,
I only spend a hundred a weekend. —
when I get to a bill — I quit.

The thief didn't really care what the crackhead had to say
but then the thief said the thief said
Then you're not really a crackhead.

Shit, I've been telling them that all along.
Now watch my back while I hit this
Then
I'm out.

CABEZA BACKWARDS

Some poems will never be captured
Be thought then gone forever
This isn't rapture
Only a fracture of my cabeza backwards
If I spit this shit with enough confidence
Will you lick it
Dig it
Spit it

TRYNA' FIND REALNESS

And the truth is I don't know how much I'm gutter truth human
And the truth is I don't know if any of these poems are fire

The truth is
I still can't balance my introvert extrovert
The truth is I still just love sunlight and music

And I really meant it when I said and wrote down
I don't know if anyone loves anyone anymore.

The truth is each of these trains that roar past my window
can feel like one hundred chances I'd never take missed
The truth is I hate dwelling in weakness
and writing of it is lame
But I'm tryna' find realness

"You can't feel the sun's ray on this overcrowded train"
That's what the deaf mute was trying to say

the tentative title
"TRYNA FIND RICHNESS"

GNUOYYRUF

Tryna
Find
Richness

X THOUGHT

To write a poem
Or to have a conversation
To attempt a conversation
On a train
With a stranger

Locked in a prison cell
X thought about views from trains
and how in the reflection of the window
X profile was righteous
Straight ahead eyes that didn't bounce when they hit you
X feeling so sharp you could put it through a needle

Inside a mind is peace not hard to find
But outside desire
Consequence
Chance

THE POSSUM

Different minds think different
Some smoke pot to get hot
Others flow from a tree
He he

Hear ye! –
I'm holding a stick
Ho, ho! You dumb
For once I'm having some fun
Pissin' in a trough like I'm George Jones

PRISON ART

Surrounded by artwork of prisoners
In a mood to write this
Vibes one of those
Surrounded by elements
Zero embellishments
Nothing is devilish
Nothing is heaven sent
Just life, just life

In and out the struggle
With or without the struggle
Trees, crows, crosses
Light beams, guitars
Praying hands and Africa

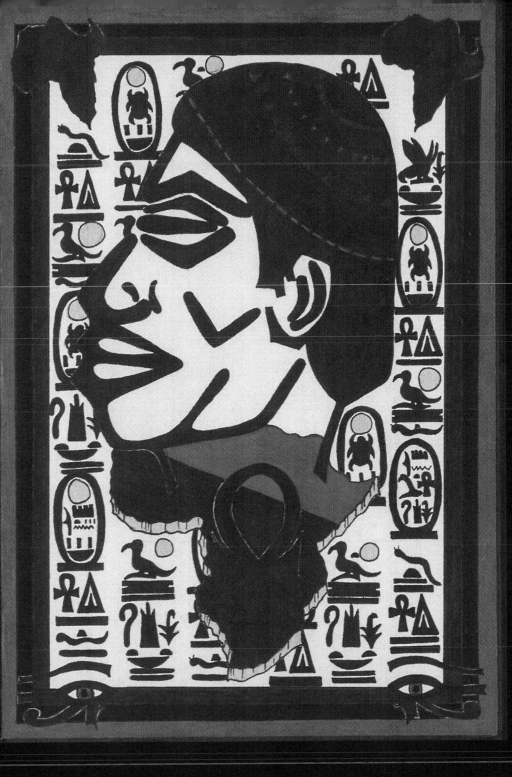

RASTA RABBI

Oh how you feel change upon you
The days press into faces
And the tires of life tread on you

Closing your eyes
and looking at old
but recent photographs
Remind you to count your blessings
and to stretch your legs and stay your own self

Because your new self is your old self
You can't wholesale up your whole self

In fact
None of that
Booby trap can fuck with that
You're an old timer
A lady lifer
A great rhymer in a cypher
And yes for two secs you even gave up self-deprecation

Jewish Jamaican
Eyes recent
But ancient

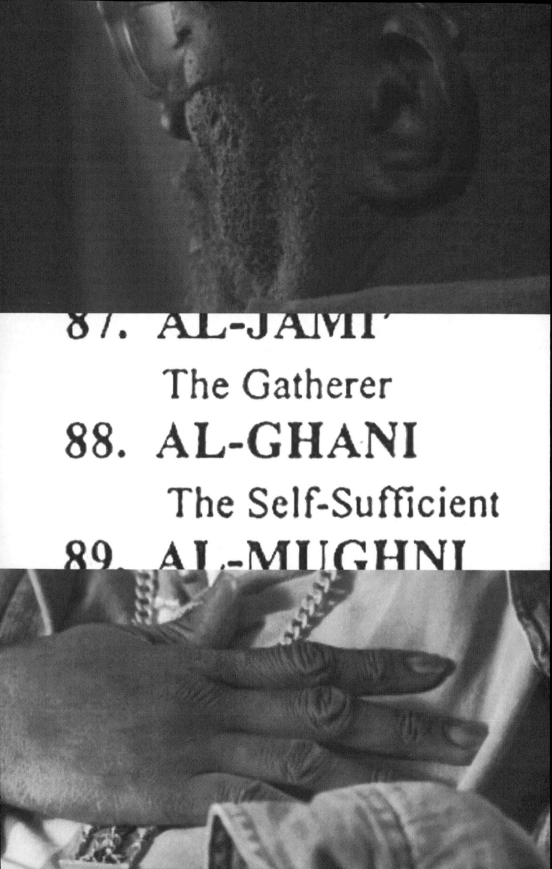

87. AL-JAMI'

The Gatherer

88. AL-GHANI

The Self-Sufficient

89. AL-MUGHNI

AL-GHANI

Pridgen passed
Pridgen's glance
Pridgen's poem about a tractor trailer full of chips
Making leap year jump over the moon
Putting July in June

Pridge it wasn't too soon
You're an alive womb
I have by heart your every move
Left side was paralyzed
Made your actions exclamation point

We could just sit on a bench
by sparrows bathing
And it would be a great adventure
Wheel you to the river

Chinatown's potholes
Ancient coolie's smoking
Their cigs on crouched knees
like wallabies

Your passing feels natural
You're my guardian angel
And towards the end of your physical life
We used to tell each other "I love you" more

You're an old gospel
Give life to the hospital
Eyes divergent lightbulbs

Right hand fat and strong
Your left was crippled frozen
A claw for peace

That stored napkins
And realness
88 days a week

"I'mma treat my ass to a bench."

that's not the only instinct
that's not the only instinct
that's not the only instinct
HAT'S NOT THE ONLY
INSTINCT

All I want to be
is hateful
Right now.
I've spent three years
Being trying to love
All I want to be
is
I've spent a lot of time
Trying to love
All I want to be
is honest and temporary like this
I mean if I stayed like this
I'd surely
It took a jugernot
To raise a mountain
And it took a boat of broken china
To

I don't know
And it took a boat of broken china
To revive the sea
All I want to be
is hateful
Right now
I've spent too much time
Trying to love.

5/9/15

HATEFUL RIGHT NOW

All I want to be
Is hateful
Right now
I've spent three years
Being
Trying
To love

All I want to be
Is
I've spent a lot of time
Trying to love

All I want to be is
Honest and temporary
I mean if I stay like this
I'd surely

It took a juggernaut
To raise a mountain
And it took a boat of broken china
To
I
Don't know
And it took a boat of broken china
To revive the sea

All I want to be
Is hateful
Right now
I've spent too much time
Trying to love.

DONE POPPED OFF

I don't need no heat on these streets
I don't need no
God
Damn
War.

JUST TO KEEP YOU SATISFIED

Listened to Marvin today
"Just To Keep You Satisfied"
"...Though the many happy times we had
Could never really
Outweigh the bad..."

Slept because I didn't wanna live
Then went to a porn film festival
I don't know what sex is like
I want to explore my sexual side
Is anyone at peace with that?
Yeah, some peeps is at peace with that
Singles ready to fuck in Brooklyn
I mean that's what it said in the ad

But now I'm just lyin' in bed
Eating peanut butter whatever
This is an amateur poem
And my life's an amateur no
I'm to blame for all of this
All my friends are in prison

I wish I was a porn star without a face
You know what I'm talking about
But probably you don't know me
So how the hell you supposed to get off on this

There goes a cumshot for the undertow
A belly flop for the sidewalk parade
An evening for the after flow
A shatter in the dungeon trap

Ceiling fan
Bubble cake
Neon man
What can you take from me?
A wider wrench?
An even plane?
I'm telling you
You're telling me

I'm an amateur philosopher
Lying feeble in this modern world
Thinking about an old man who was once a porn actor
Whose cray days are nay today
But ay porn acting crayzay?
Are you a top or a ba ba atom?
I wanna get creative with some
one
I always get creative with my
self
And I'm not talking about sex
I'm talking about making music with my hands
And growing what I understand

But I'm feeble I'm an old porn star 'cept I never acted in a porn
I've gone — this is one of my turns
I'm an applesnake
You are a burn
I've gone
10,000 miles without walking into something that moved me
And chewed me up in the undertow —

I've gone.
10,000 miles in a bible character's shoes
Just to find out god and the devil were both fucking
Bad news
I'm here —
10,000 miles away from the blues

Until the blues walked in and met me
at a sidewalk parade
Under some slim shade
Eating a fist naked
and a very very sacred
Tuna fish sandwich

Now I'm walking in the sidelines of the sidewalk parade
I'm heading to the dungeon trap with a wider wrench to fix the
    ceiling fan
I bumped into a neon man and broke his whole body
I'm fighting for an even plane but I know that life's a bubble cake
    and pops easily
I'm looking for a bubble butt like the one in the picture that said
"Single and ready to fuck in Brooklyn"

I'm a joke, a hypotenuse, I'm ready to fuck in Brooklyn
But the ad is a scam you KNOW the ad is a scam
And the adman looks like Dracula on Beverly Hills with plastic
    surgery
And must have been ugly to start with

A family man a housewife
In whose world?
Those don't exist no more
Or do they or mid-century or
Bullshit

I'm shrinking to the size of an ordinary peanut
I'm not well hung or wel-come
The only thing I am is well dumb
And I dropped you a line
you fell off the face of the earth –

I hope you're havin' a good time
on Saturn's rings

VIGILANTE LINES

Vertical studs and voluntary pain
I feel a maelstrom ahead of me
Vigilante line
Rise n' shine bandit
Permanent mud
Kisses that shocked the censors

I'm all woman and I need a man to make me come alive
Bed crazy, too much SEX on the beaches?

Is
Love
GOOD for your heart?
A cure for homosexuals?
How Elvis stays on top.

TIJUANA BIBLE

Got a Tijuana Bible in my left hand
Cum on the other
I just left Comstock
headed to the Everard Baths

But some mayor closed it in '86
so I blew up the Society for the Suppression of Vice
Put me in the last glory hole in Manhattan
Gonna name my kid Echo

Scientist sees a duck fuck duck
other duck is dead
Due to an attempted rape flight
Scientist wins an award for that

J BEAUTY GIRL

Past the midnight hour
J train coming home
Beauty girl beauty girl
Across with tall socks boots on
Goal in life to talk to her
and not in a creep way
Goal in life to talk to her
and not in no creep way
Man she poetry in motion
on this fuckin' train
I bet she's going home
She's somebody's daughter
Several people love her
She's been twenty eight people's lover
That bitch ain't no motherfucker

FOR A LONER

This is a poem for a loner
Who wishes she wasn't
Just like every other poem

Ever written

WASHED UP

I'm older now
I've become a gay icon
Blind fisted morons get jealous of my two step
I'm sexist
I'm racist
I can't get laid
And you call yourself a poet?
Ha! Then get up and go
Go out naked in the sunset
Dumb bitch

Modelo
I use it as a candle holder on my windowsill
Take this pill line flow
I'm in prison in the pill line
I am mentally ejected
I am high on perfection
I'm having a C-section
And I love you Sophia you doula
Look you just baptized me in poet's water and I spit it out

I'm goin' down south
I'm rapid fire motherfucker
My daddy fucked my uncle
Sidetrack

This a bubble butt mindset
Priceless fuck a rhyme
I'm in the tap of a buddha

Ms. Soloway
She was an english teacher in high school
I read Sartre and listened to The Cure
The same time Leon Benson read Nausea at Wabash
How hilarious how beautiful is that?
Clap back 'rade!

I'm seeing my soul in a vision of realness
Inhibition derailed it's a new day
Come carry on
And get on this fuckin train.

Do you see how we can turn beauty into nothing
I mean nothingness into beauty?

Shoot me on a stage glittered red and see-through
Like some Hollywood idol — oh, fuck that

I remember dumb times on Hollywood and Vine
Nah, they weren't dumb you were just learning how to

Shyne
Remember him huh
Is that dude still in prison?
Do you still have a subscription to F.E.D.S. magazine?
Yo you mad ghetto
No I'm a chameleon in the undertow
Krayzie Bone
is my favorite
T-H-U-G WE BE –

I aint no thug
I just like rest in peace signs
Dig mine
This shit Tish was writ in 6 or 7 minutes
I'm finished
I'm excited for Monique to get out of prison

And Leon Benson
And all you other souldias
Hold on
I'm gonna fight for you
That's the deal dun

Point blank.
I got that from Tameca Cole – shout out
I got you baby girl
for a take out of that IHOP
Nah I could do better than that
plus I just named a corporation
I'm writing this naked
It's like 6 in the morning
A few minutes ago I was mourning
My last girlfriend
Who I still love n' always will
Real talk maine

You well oh you that is a whole a 'nother poem
You make me think of riddles like skittles on little noodles
Toodles
That's what these bitches used to say to me
As goodbye
And fuck the word bitch unless a snitch just tricked the licorice box
That's such a bad flavor
"Short nigga but my dick is long"
I wrote that in a strip club below this several months ago

Okay now
For real
I am coming to the end of the fuck
I'm becoming a Hollywood franchise at this fucking point it's boring
But I'm not gonna

Hey
Remember that T.S. Eliot poem it took five years to write?

Guess what
So did this
This is shit
That's the shit
Suck my

Take that back.
Not tryna' disrespect my generation.

several months ago
Okay now
For real I am coming to
the end of the fuck
I am becoming a hollywood
franchise at this fucking point
It's boring
But I'm not gonna
Hey
Remember that T.S. Eliot poem,
that it took him five years to write
Guess what
So did this
This is shit
That's the shit
Suck my ——
I take that back
I'm not tryna disrespect my
generation.

PLUMMETING

Plummeting into darkness is not a good feeling
Being uninspired is not a good feeling
Never talking to strangers is not a good feeling
Writing the same poem a hundred times is not a good feeling

NO FOOD

No food could make me hungry
No food could solve my hunger now
I could fuck a thousand gales
And no pussy would feel like yours
I could fuck a thousand guys
And no pussy would feel like yours

I dream of you believable
Achievable in distance
That one day I'll retreat to you
And love you like a piston

No food could quench my hunger
'sides the food that is your love and hate
While you have such less hate than me
I bring it out of your synergy

And I heard the lyrics as all I want
is to hold you like an animal
Just to be with you again
Just to hold you like a dog

BETTY WRIGHT'S
FOUR LETTER WORD

What's on my mind
Thinking about my friend who just got married
That was like his only serious girlfriend
said his old friend to me
Lots of one night stands
then her

And becoming more face value
was inking on that too
I am becoming
Less and less bullshit

Of course you too
I guess every heartbreak sharpens you
or each pain that's natural
will lessen your bullshit
See your life as more of a full clip though

I don't know if you broke it
But you did are and will
cause me PAIN
Betty Wright's four letter word.

You know that soul singer?
rocked "From Pain to Joy"
"No Pain No Gain"
"After the Pain"

Man I love her voice
Her style
but boy her lyrics
They're just so old school
when it comes to femininity

Talkin' about
"Don't blame Mr. Charlie
Mr. Charlie is just a man
And he's doing the best he can…
I heard 'em say – "

She's always talking about she's the clean up woman
"Girls you can't do what the guys do, no.
And still be a lady, no…
no no no no."

You're on some non-bracket type shit
defining your sex as a woman of 23 moons
You take pride in saying you're a slut
you have some fascination with that

We grew up in the generacin' where porno was a click away

I was looking at this old newspaper from 1953
and everything in it was so precise and straight forward
They ain't have instant connection then and they didn't have net
    pornos
But who knows? Maybe we're all more realer now
Maybe it's a balance act let's see who makes it to the finish line

You'll never finish mine
O.D. rocker monkey on my back
Man you made it what went wrong?
Just too many back stabs?
It all became so heavy walkin' around umbrella and a gas mask

Now I'm tipsy and I should stop but I wanna rhyme lap dance
I have a 7am call time tomorrow in Manhattan
Fall time
I'll think about you Miss Energy
on the subway in the morning
Bopping your head in bed
Naked to my song

Our real interesting day together
Our last our last our over
Our dynamics crimson and clover.

Sir I ain't touched my cell
my cell phone all day
And in one tap when I set that alarm it'll reset my energy
Tell me if you called me text messaged me tagged me
See there's that part of love that's fat and wants to keep eating and
     eating
up the compliments
Eat my love

As I cook my own feast
gonna put on that Chains song
That one about say goodbye don't follow

"Say goodbye don't follow..."

NUDE BEACH

Damn right woman
Go out topless in the sun
Run into the water
You are what you've become
Your breastesses ain't taboo
and neither a penis too
Let's stop acting like fools
and get into a mood
I am a lone ranger
but I love the idle stranger
I am a solitary
man often just a laymen man
Always a creatin' man
Soon to be a journey man
Scripture in a heart a' gold
Live for two men three men fold
He man she man
Wrestling super demons
Rollin' on a tire on barb wire
'Til the end!

DEAR 2PAC

Ey Pac –

I'm about to see a play inspired by you
The lights are going down now
Sittin' next ta two honeys you would've talked to

I just turned 25
The age you were when you died
and during this intermission I'm wondering if you had an
    introverted side
A real mover and shaker
who new how to party
Had a lot of guts
You spoke for so many
There would've been another like you
just they wouldn'ta been as multi-facet
They wouldn't have wrote Dear Mama
and then Wonda Why They Call U Bitch

You June baby like me
Jokerman like me
Energy thing like me
but with a bit more bravery

We need cats like you Pac
I see you rapping in heaven
Miles on the sax
Jam Master on the beatbox –

Spent the mornin' on the corner chill with John Donne n'
Jackie Wilson came around to show us love poppin'
Was the hoochies on the ave, thug poets rockin'
Tradin' verses fulla' curses when 2pac dropped in
God heard me holla'd — Who that balla' wit tha thug passion?!
Fienda' ask him for a class in how he done rappin! —
Said God in due respect U gotsta chill family
I neva give away the secrets that I been plannin!
But won't ya come with me down ta thugz mansion?
And U can judge me as I am —
A soul dancin'.

RIKERS ISLAND

We waited eternity for the man in the grey suit
D.O.C. on the back to walk in
Man I saw that dude a few weeks ago
Khesan was rockin' a leather

He's there on a trumped up charge
It was his jacket that got him there
Not the leather, talkin' crime record
Robbed a bank with a note
Fed time
Some fed joint in West VA where they sent him

He was a year out doing good then got accused of a burglary
Now he's back on the island, building OBCC
'parently that's where the baddest crabs go

We're all crabs in a barrel
They keep throwing more on the pile
We're beautiful crabs some of us
With big butts freckles and dreads
some a broken leg
a toddler in tow
a tank top –

YOU CAN'T COME IN WITH THAT.
Put on this 4XL shirt.

And when four enter the visit room
ten more walk in
Visitors endless

Couple days to Christmas
Asked a regular if that was why she said
"Nah it's always like this."

Almost all of us were black or brown
We almost all had interesting faces
We were nameless and famous and shameless
Shameful and waiting and waiting
Some to be sentenced
Some to have a retrial
Some to go home
Home home home...
or 10 or 20 or
Rest of life upstate.

The families were waiting
The friends were waiting
The lifers upstate were waiting
For you to walk in.
The balance was waiting
The visit room was waiting
The next crab barrel was waiting
Waiting for something positive.

The man in the grey suit arrived
Man that visit just flew
And I saw that lifeful youngster
who ran up to his daddy

On the subway later
going back to Brooklyn
I saw the lifeful youngster
with his mommy on the platform.
Said "that's the lady with the baby
I just saw with daddy."

THUG MOTIVATION
for South Carolina 9 and all victims of blind hate
written to "Rivers Have Songs" by gHSTS & gUITARS

I need some thug motivation Right Now.
This is a thing for nine shot dead in a church.
The shooter a young white supreme shit
The victims of a darker
skin

Hey Harriet,
Why don't they put your face on the twenty?
They're talking about it, you hear?
And if money exists
Might as well have a soulyah on there

This is for
Well, I told you who this is for
9 deal souls who just lit up a room
1 dead soul just darkened a corner
Well he's alive he's just in a cage now
Huh what'll they do with him
Us and them

I saw two figures in the night
trying to steal the gaslight
They rode a pick up truck
confederate decal on the dashboard
License and registration?
This car belongs to Slim Jim Crow
Okay sir, carry on then
Enjoy your evening officer

We'll keep this our little bonding,
We'll keep this between you and me
In this supremashit town
Where a few would kill 'em a black, yeah

I guess that kind of hatred's something I'll never understand
I'm just a person
I want to lend a hand
I'm just a breather
I didn't put myself here
I'm a million different things
I'm just trying to live
I don't have any kids
but one day I'll have one

This is because
Rivers have songs.
Because those nine are gonna live on
And when my child is born
We're gonna walk down to that river
and remember
We're gonna walk with ghosts and guitars
and they'll play us sweet melodies

I said to start I need some thug motivation
Right Now.
Should I explain
In this world I know I have to.
I don't mean I need Young Jeezy the trap rap on blast
I don't mean anything having to do with some silly stereotype
Where an ig'nant supremacist would say yeah that's what black
    people are like

Thug motivation
Just a will to keep going
As an outlaw, a poet, oh lord that's pretentious
As an outlaw, a forest, a sparrow on a subway,

a disabled man on a runway
I'm not a matador or his cape

Shout out to the lifers

I am we are you are
I are we are you
going in circles
and I love it
must this end

No cuz rivers have songs
And the music is beautiful goes on....

Breathe.
I stopped breathing
See my child is teething
And I won't de-nail this cat
it's learning to play the xylophone

Don't you see all creatures have beauty
Makes me think of the guy in solitary
who made best friends with a mouse
and used his hair as a leash to walk it about

Today I got a letter from a man who may never get out of prison
He criticized gays and gender change, called me a new generation
This man I hold high esteem for
and I wanted to include him in this
Because in so many ways this creature is goodness

I am a creature that's ruthless
And I too have goodness
So much
And I have a hunch
back you know

Back in the days of
The present day of
Now
Show some respect

Yeah you
There's enough hate to go around
Why don't you burn that flag down at City Hall?
Or just take it down
m'am.

Hatred is just the love of a child forsaken
It's not gonna go away by stuffing your face in front of a box
And if there's white trash there's black trash so fuck all of that

I said this is a mountain of realness
Climb it
This is my walking shoes
On a singing river

HOTEL NEXT TO WAFFLEHOUSE

EconoLodge
Eating bean dip
can that looks like cat food
I'm afraid of Americans
This place has no clog on the bathtub

No one can take baths
or kill themselves
Wanna do both

I lived in a place like this

BORING ASS AMERICAN

Don't worry
You boring ass American
I'm not
Gonna tread on you.

DON'T WANT
AN OPINION
JUST WANT
THE RAW FEELING
P   U   T
THE RECORD   ON
D R O P
THAT BASS LINE
D R O P
THAT HI – HAT
N O W
WE'RE TALKING

YEAH

Don't want
An opinion
Just want
The raw feeling
Put
The record on
Drop
That bass line
Drop
That hi-hat
Now
We're talking

And you know it's hard to
be rocknroll all the time,
Yeah you wrote that one,
remember?
Yeah you wrote that once,
remember?

GREETINGS from OHIO

You

beautiful

beatiful man

ROCK N' ROLL ALL THE TIME

Shaking off all this half baked poetry and just coming out with
    the truth
It's hard to stay rock n' roll
All the time.

Things are gonna get in the way
Dull shy energies
Ox n' moron enemies
Diet baby food

A real rock n' roller
Loves the music in life
Not just on wax or live
But in the sea lion sparrow
Crow cow ox
N' sometimes even the moron
Or is there no
Music in the moron?

The rock n' roller will get lost in the music
Really so often and let it do her talking
and her commitment
and roll with the punches

The rock must strive to find and be realness
Surrounded by hundreds of strangers
Inland on an island
On a layover flight in an airport
Still tryna' to feel like rolling
To feel some kind of pride
Some passion rolling rock
N' roll ain't just a genre

one genre Soul
Rap Jazz Classical
Reggae Folk Industrial
Basking in raw power
No siempre y solamente
Music.

You rockers know what I'm saying

It's performing like all your doubts
Are bullshit which they are
It's blowing your own mind every time
Its taken its toll on nothing —
It rejuvenates

It's the most important thing in your life
What makes you from a depressed shish kebab
To a revelatory renegade
Getting naked in front of strangers
And it comes out automatic.

And that's the that that
oughta foreclose bull
SHIT that's jive
JIVE.
Right on man! Outta sight!
Alright.

Now you might look back on these words one day
"Man but I paid the price."
You might get backstabbed so many times you won't have any
    skin left
You might become a lunatic or you might get rhino skin
Who knows?

Who's next

Please please I want to
keep feeling alive. I never
realized how hard you gotta
fight for that, for me that
is, I have to fight.
... i got to testify...
    i got to testify...

BLUUUU-O-OOOOOHS)
BLUUUUUU-U-OOOOOHS)

I GOT TO TESTIFY

I GOT TO TESTIFY

BLU
BLU   U-OOOOOHS,"
                     UU-OOOOOHS,"

I GOT   TO TESTIFY
I GOT   TO TESTIFY
                     OOOOO

ROXIE

Kissing you is a conversation
At the end of the world

Love be an unsure thing
Love be an I want more thing
Love stay searching
Love stay lurking
Trying to pry a door down

I'm constantly, well often, thinking about you now
And we ain't even made love yet
We ain't even fucked yet

We ain't even seen
One another in daylight
Ain't even had a meal together
Yet you feel like a butterfly

A friend and lover I kiss
Invisibly before I sleep
— What the fuck?
Do I fall so so so
easily

Am I seeking your validation
Body and energy
O please be the latter
I don't want to be bullshit

Roxie
Come on

LOVE AIN'T REAL

"I wanna know if love is wild
I wanna know if love is real..."
- Springsteen

What the fuck is love?
Love ain't real
To answer Bruce's question
Love ain't real

Talkin' bout romantic love
Bend over backwards love
Smitten fucking kitten love
That shit ain't real

That shit exist in your youth
Now that shit ain't real
Now it's a raw deal
That boy is just a mouth

With a southern guillotine
That love ain't real
Maybe one in a thousand
People find that someone
But that new lover a' yours
That's all she is
A lover

You fuck her
Don't think for a minute
It gets much deeper'n that
Even if she falling for you
Your lives not fit

You know that that's why
You're not falling back

You know that lovey dovey
Thing is done with

You want a constant challenge
Alright then find it

HARD WORKER

Sometimes alone in my room at night
Think I hear my roommate rub one out
It's not a bad sound
She told me last time her heart beat like butterfly

There was some punk band with a song
called "Don't Call Me White"
I think about that and laugh in my head
Not outward but softly in my head

If I'm any race it's a race against waste.
If I'm any history it's Two Strike from Mannahatta.

Now some Native American rights group would kill me
Squash me for being outlandish
Oh I'm outlandish?
Oh life has balance?
Yeah fuck you I thought so I mean kill them with kindness

Doc picked up Juliette the other day
His daughter, it was beautiful
I loved seeing them together
It was harmony, it was the cure

I'm tired of relationships that don't know where they're going
Like Two Strike I feel sudden
Like Two Strike I am simple
And every wrinkle on my head's a wrinkle in time

This is a tired
Hard Worker

WHITE SHITILEGE

I am not a white savior
All that shit is bullshit
I have nothing to prove
Except for things completely unrelated
To being a white savior

I don't wish I were black
I don't wish I were anything
I yam what I yam like Popeye
And yeah I like spinach

I don't toss and turn
In my head about white shitilege
I know my place in this world
The time I could read and philosophize about it
Could also be spent doing something good in it

That thought reminds me of Mark Springer
My friend who is a lifer
Who says the moment he stops doing
Is the moment he starts dying.

I am Fury Young
My given name is Yuvi Brozgold
Man I haven't written that in so long

My great grandpa owned a poultry shop
On Rivington and Clinton
He was poor but he was smart
He believed in education

His daughter's the hardest
working person I know
Man sometimes I wonder if that work ethic comes from repression
But then I keep going
Cuz I guess I've got to do it

a Real HIGH maintenance
Forever

Some kid from THE Beary
STARTS LETTIN LOOSE
BUT HE GETS BLOWN RIGHT
OUT OFF IS FEET

SOME LIVES
YOU
DON'T
FORGET

"GET
WERE
THEY
JUST
LOST
IN
IT"

REAL FOOD

Feel like a fuckin' tweakhead
A tweaker
Thought the train was pullin' in but it was leaving
Least I got a free ride cuz I hopped that train in a hurry
A jiffy
I'm skippy
The only thing not flowing is my whip release
And for that I'm balanced like Hitler getting fisted
Please let the extended play see the ethers of brilliancy
Let avocado spaceships get rid of this tax man silence
Yeah you guessed it I'm on the J
Yeah you guessed it I'm on the train

Tomahawk back
With more nicknames than that rapper from the 9th ward
I'm Bloody, Project Tyrant, Two Strike from Mannahatta
I'm Y
U
B
I
BOO YA

Right now this silence golden as I slip into multidentity
I'm sent to be leading the army of realness in sentencing
Ain't takin' no shorts cuz it's way too late to stop now.

Lockdown.
I don't wanna hear about that scenery
The only chains you're in be the ones called Mickey D's.
And even those you callin' quits because you fienda' cook up some
REAL FOOD.

THIS IS WHAT THE
LOVE OF GOD MEANS

Poem in the Bedford Hills visit room
On a pocket Bible table of contents
This place will make you realistic

Woman in state green heads back to unit
Says to C.O. "Get home safe!"
Big smile

Drove up here with Apostle
They wouldn't let her in cuz of prior
She called them the enemy

Here comes Valerie

Peace in the World

MEAT & MILK

"Got to get off this machine."
Said some angel in San Francisco
Somewhere in Brooklyn
A poet sat waiting
Was it a poet or a pot with a lot to piss in
That didn't matter
It was the stroke of mystery
Whistling

Tell me tomahawk
What is pain now
It's not real because
Holding on ain't a side effect
It's everything

Though eternal questions
is a ticket to ride?

There's something in the light
Switch of your fantasies
That takes you away
To when torture was medieval

What I'm tryna say is
The effort that's put into it
What I'm tryna pray for is
The freedom of a praying man

There comes a time
You take a breath from your workload

See you've become
Evolved and still deprecating

You feel the old fears you set aside while distracted
You hold on to the edge of the cliff because it keeps you on balance
You think of times uninhibited
Raw rough raging rhinoceros
Yoga in a group naked
After the pain on the subway

Getting off this machine
Playing this black guitar
Feeling some horizon
Take it back

To that Ridge Street love affair
Her grandfather was a coolie
She came three times and drooled even

There needed to be some symmetry
Like a set of bongos
Not forbid your E=energy
Return to the precipice
Spit three times and drool on it
I'm not talking about that meat and milk

"I never thought about
not making it.

But the it has nothing
to do with show business

The it I'm trying to
make is me.
Who am I?"

Richard Pryor
'71

LEARN CHINESE - Cook
做(zuò)菜(cài)
Lucky Numbers 46, 22, 25, 51, 6, 19

* LICK
1. open 5th

CAPO o7
3rd fret
CAMPAIGNER: D. Gmaj7. D. Bmin
G. F#. Bmin. A. Bmin. G. A. [*].

HATS OFF

I'd like to thank my parents for creating me and then seeing me through. I'd like to thank my brother for being a writing inspiration and critic, who sat through almost every poem in this book and either nodded or gave feedback, and sometimes said, "cut it." Alexander Pridgen. Everyone on Die Jim Crow. All the people in this book. All my friends and family.

Deep gratitude goes to Lit Riot Press and to Benjamin Taylor for taking a chance on me, seeing me through the process, and working through the graphics.

Thanks to all the musicians and artists who inspire me, you, and us. Thanks to Spoon Jackson, the Knight of Realness — my Peace Gang 'rade.

Thanks to everyone who wrote blurbs for this book: Master Lee, Abiodun Oyewole, Alex Tatarsky, Judith Tannenbaum ("some angel in San Francisco"), and Gabrielle David. Thanks to Mickey Hoover for putting the pe'ot on the poet.

Thanks to Dave Jones for the cover photo and cover graphic work (and remember to drink Fury-Cola). Thanks to Brian Goodwin for the author photos, and Ciera Wells-Jones for the chassid outfit.

Last, not least, thank you to all the strangers who still make me question this life like a kid of fewer moons.

Fury Young
October 2016

ART & PHOTO CREDITS

All handwritten pages and artwork by Fury Young, unless noted below.

p. 20 - handwritten poem by Fury Young and Spoon Jackson.
p. 21 - Fury Young and Spoon Jackson. Photo by Richard Tell.
p. 63 – Lower East Side mural by Chico. Photo by Fury Young.
p. 89 – Fury and notebook. Photo by Brian Goodwin.
p. 94 – Alexander Pridgen. Photo by Christopher Cafaro.
p. 124 – Fury and Alex. Photo by Lee Brozgol.
p. 127 – Fury and Alex 2. Photo by Lee Brozgol.
p. 143 – Tameca Cole. Photographer unknown.
p. 145 – Spoon Jackson. Photographer unknown.
p. 163 – "Back to Life" drawing by Obadyah Ben-Yisrayl.
p. 164 – Untitled drawing by Spoon Jackson.
p. 166 – Screenshots from film "Pridgen" (2009) photographed by Christopher Cafaro and directed by Fury Young.
p. 217 – Valerie Seeley. Photographer unknown.

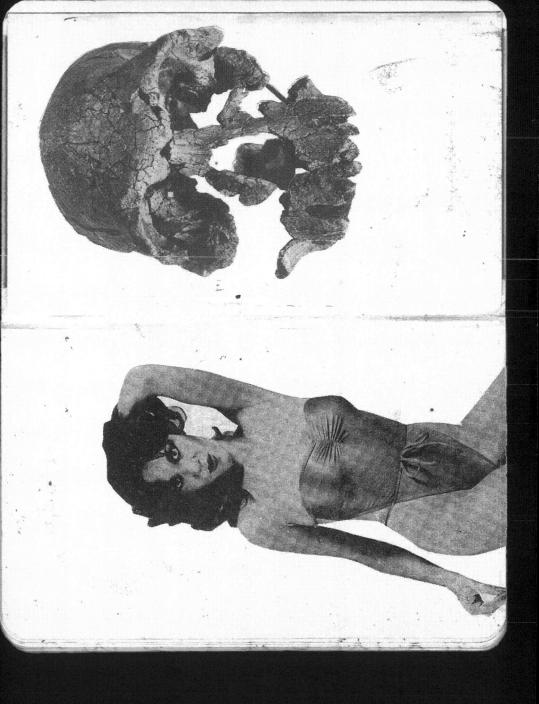

ABOUT THE AUTHOR

Fury Young is a poet/musician from the Lower East Side of Manhattan. *Meat & Milk* is his first book of poetry. In addition to his solo work, Young is currently producing a music project called *Die Jim Crow*, a concept album about racism in the U.S. prison system written and performed by formerly and currently incarcerated black musicians from across the country. Fury works as a carpenter to pay the bills while juggling his many projects. He lives in Brooklyn, New York.

For more information:
www.furyyoung.com
www.diejimcrow.com

Made in the USA
Columbia, SC
09 December 2018